CW01475694

GIRL ON THE
Gangway
A TRAVEL WRITER'S TALE

DC WISHART

CRUISE-PLUS PUBLISHING
Troon, United Kingdom

Copyright © 2015 by DC Wishart.

All rights reserved. No part of this publication may be reproduced, distributed or transmitted in any form or by any means, including photocopying, recording, or other electronic or mechanical methods, without the prior written permission of the publisher, except in the case of brief quotations embodied in critical reviews and certain other noncommercial uses permitted by copyright law. For permission requests, write to the publisher, addressed "Attention: Permissions Coordinator," via the dcwishart.com website below.

Cruise-Plus Publishing
cruise-plus.com
dcwishart.com
Publisher's Note: This is a work of fiction. All names, characters, places, and incidents are a product of the author's imagination. Locales and public names are sometimes used for atmospheric purposes. Any resemblance to actual people, living or dead, or to businesses, companies, events, institutions, or locales is completely coincidental.

Ordering Information:
Quantity sales. Special discounts are available on quantity purchases by corporations, associations, and others. For details, contact the "Special Sales Department" at the address above.

Girl on the Gangway: A Travel Writer's Tale/ DC Wishart. — 1st ed.
ISBN 978-0-9931518-0-4

Yes, there was a girl on the gangway.
That is not fiction,
and this book is for her.

RETURN
TO
ANN

Under the wide and starry sky,
Dig the grave and let me lie.
Glad did I live and gladly die,
And I laid me down with a will.

This be the verse you grave for me:
Here he lies where he longed to be;
Home is the sailor, home from sea,
And the hunter home from the hill.

– Robert Louis Stevenson, 1850-1894,
inscribed on his tomb in a spectacular location in Samoa,
but a distant place few get to visit other than those
on South Sea cruises

ACKNOWLEDGEMENTS

Many thanks to Lee Ellis, retired US Air Force colonel and Vietnam POW, whom I met on a cruise ship from Barcelona to Ft Lauderdale.

Listening to Lee's experience of more than five years in the Hanoi Hilton and other POW camps made me realize his story (and book, *Leading with Honor*), and mine (to a much lesser degree), have a role in understanding what men, and women, went through in the war that cost 58,220 American lives.

I was also encouraged by Robert W. Bone, one of America's best-loved travel writers, author of *Fire Bone!* and other travel books, and given assistance by Haig Gordon, Alan Dirkin and Peter Brookes.

Finally, I wish to acknowledge Ruth Schwartz, aka the Wonderlady, who with skill, patience and humor helped birth this newspaperman's first novel, bringing forth a handsome book, professionally designed and formatted and available for sale around the world.

TABLE OF CONTENTS

AUTHOR'S INTRODUCTION

I have been a roving journalist all my life, but mostly I was in Canada, where I quit my job as travel editor of the *Vancouver Sun* to go to Oxford University (celebrity chef Rick Stein and I went up about the same time as mature students) and en route took a cruise — on the first voyage of the *Royal Viking Star*, a sensational new ship that invented modern, luxury cruising.

Since then I have done more than 200 sailings as a cruise writer, many of them inaugurals out of American ports as the cruise industry grew quickly, initially in vessels with around 500 passengers, minnows compared to today's mega-ships with upwards of 6000 on board.

My companions were a select band of reporters who were well looked after, but there was more to it than the first-class air travel and champagne in the cabin. Small ships are very sociable and as a VIP group we were invited to parties every night — by the captain, chief engineer, hotel manager, cruise director, even the doctor. Ships' doctors also had parties for MDs on board, for if there was a medical emergency at sea they wanted to know which cabin to call for a cardiologist or an anesthetist.

Gossip flowed as fast as the alcohol and it was often about sex. We heard about wealthy women passengers on board to meet their lovers, usually barmen or waiters (in port they would walk hand in hand) while on one cruise a mother and daughter team seduced young crewmen every night — in the same cabin — then sought me out in the bar one evening, not for a threesome, but just to tell me what they were up to. Presumably the motivation was the notion there is something liberating about sharing intimate secrets.

And of course we were at sea, where people used to, and still do, let their hair down with the same abandon as what happens in Vegas, stays in Vegas.

As I did cruise after cruise, saw the seven seas, went down to Antarctica, up the Amazon, along the Nile, to the Galapagos and more, I could see a book in the making, but it needed more than wild sex and gags about the midnight buffet.

Then, 20 years ago, I sailed on a remarkable voyage from Hong Kong to Singapore.

This is now a busy cruise route with popular ports of call in Vietnam, but back then President Bill Clinton was working on but had not concluded normalizing diplomatic relations with the Hanoi government — despite objections that American prisoners of war were still being held captive.

Our ship was not a swanky new vessel, but the Ocean Pearl, an old Baltic ferry that had pioneered cruises to China. Among the passengers on this sailing was a handful of American pilots who had flown combat missions in the Vietnam war, including Cole Black, a US Navy pilot who had been shot down and held prisoner in the infamous Hanoi Hilton.

We did not know what to expect when we got to Saigon, newly named Ho Chi Minh City. One passenger, a Vietnamese woman returning with her American husband, was so afraid she never left the ship, while others, including the press naturally, partied in the Apocalypse Bar on the Saigon River.

She reminded me of a woman we had seen on another cruise ship. "Who's that girl on the gangway?" said one of my journalist colleagues as we boarded. We later learned that the strikingly attractive woman was the wife of another US Navy pilot shot down over Vietnam. He was MIA — missing in action. She was a woman with her life on hold.

This then is my book, dedicated to that woman, and how I would have liked her journey to end.

DC Wishart
Troon, United Kingdom
December 2014

CHAPTER 1
On board the aircraft carrier
Kitty Hawk,
off the coast of Vietnam

<u>March 1972</u>

Commander Jim Robertson, also known as Doc, bent his lanky frame as he walked into the tiny cabin on the aircraft carrier Kitty Hawk. "Morning, Rupert," he said to the skeleton, complete with aviator sunglasses and wings, that stood in a corner. "No flying today, chum," Rupert was informed as Doc sat down and reached for a stack of paperwork. From above there was a cascade of sounds from the flight deck.

There was a big raid on. The Vietnam War would be over in a year but in the meantime the Navy continued to send its jets deep into North Vietnam to support ground forces. Ever since the Kitty Hawk, a huge floating fortress with 5000 crew, had arrived at its battle station, three aircraft had been shot down and although all of the pilots had been rescued, several were badly shaken up. It was Doc's job to keep them flying.

Not that he had ever expected to be doing this sort of thing. Shoreside he had been a pediatrician, but his father ran a flying school, he was a qualified pilot, and there was a war on. He had volunteered because he wanted to do his bit, but also there was the chance to fly fast jets.

Doc loved the thrill of being catapulted off the deck of the Kitty Hawk in a rugged, versatile F8 Crusader fighter. The aircraft in his squadron had downed several MiG aircraft the Russians supplied to the North Vietnamese, but dodging the SAM ground-to-air missiles was always a worry.

Two days ago, one had got Gordie Jones, homing on to his blazing tailpipe. Gordie knew his stuff and had thrown the Crusader around to shake off the missile, but the SAM was locked in and blew the back end off his machine, leaving Gordie to eject and parachute into hostile territory.

The Navy was ready for such situations. A rescue helicopter, which had been flying in support, was overhead in 10 minutes, much faster than the North Vietnamese Army, which sent a truck with soldiers in the general direction of Gordie's parachute. Fortunately this was in an area of rough country that made its progress slow.

Gordie spotted the helicopter, released a flare, and in seconds he was being bundled aboard the machine. "Welcome aboard," said the helicopter pilot. "Hope you don't mind if we don't stick around for a sightseeing tour.

There's a truckload of soldiers heading this way and they have your room key for the Hanoi Hilton."

The helicopter climbed quickly to 100 feet and whirled away from the direction of the truck. Gordie sighed with relief. He would not be sleeping in that infamous jail — at least not this night.

Now Gordie was back flying again. Doc had argued that the pilot should be rested but the admiral wanted him for today's attack.

There was a knock on his door. "Mail, sir," said the sailor, "Just came in from Saigon courtesy of the admiral's helicopter."

Doc thumbed through the letters. There was one from home. He sat down, pushed his cap back, and opened the letter carefully. It was from Cathy. Would there be word about a baby? Some weeks earlier he had been home on leave and this had been more than discussed.

"Doc!" His cabin door opened again, this time urgently. "Doc — you're wanted for today's mission. You're taking Gordie's place. Apparently he cracked up at the flight briefing."

Doc pushed the letter aside and ran to the crew locker room, got dressed in his G-suit and life vest, strapping on his belt with pistol and Navy survival knife and grabbed his helmet as he raced up to the flight deck. The Crusader was waiting, its engine warmed up, a crewman standing by to help him into the cockpit.

The pre-flight check complete, Doc lined up the jet on the steam catapult opened the throttle wide, waited for the signalman's arm to drop, and released the brakes.

Two seconds later he was over the Tonkin Gulf and setting course for North Vietnam.

Back in his cabin, the letter from home lay on his desk.
"My Darling," it said, "I am so happy to tell you that you
are going to be a father …"

It was a letter Doc would never see.

CHAPTER 2
Seattle

June 1982

The roar from the jet taking off from Whidbey Island air station made Cathy Robertson duck instinctively. No matter how often they came here she never quite got used to the sudden, deafening roar. Her son Tom, now a feisty nine-year-old, was just the opposite. He loved the circus of screaming jets of the sort his father flew.

Doc, his father, was what the military termed Missing in Action. The boy knew well the acronym, MIA. The war had ended nine years earlier but he had not returned. Nearly 600 captured Americans were home, but not Doc. Was he dead or alive? Nobody knew. Other pilots reported seeing Doc in the Hanoi Hilton in good health, but one day he disappeared from the prison.

Young Tom shouted excitedly as another jet screamed off the runway, hurtling over a giant billboard that read, "Excuse the noise, but it's the sound of freedom." Who came up with that guff, thought Cathy.

Where had he gone? The victorious regime in Hanoi was saying nothing.

In the meantime Cathy was effectively a widow, and a lonely one. She lived in a small town near Seattle and worked for a newspaper as its art director. It was a good job that kept her busy during the day, and she and Tom had a comfortable little cottage with a view over the Pacific. As they turned into her street a neighbor waved and gave her a warm smile. It was George. Good old George, she thought. Always there — but so was his wife.

No way, thought Cathy as she smiled back defensively. She suspected George was a risk taker and that spelled trouble in a small town. There were other men, some of them quite single, who clearly fancied her, but what could she do when her husband could walk in the front door at any time?

"Hi Cathy!" called a voice as she stopped the car at her driveway. It was Shirley, a friend from work, on her bike.

"Coming to the party tonight?"

"Mummy doesn't go to parties," said Tom as he got out of the car.

Cathy gave him a playful push and said: "Yeah right, I'm an old stick-in-the-mud."

"Tell you what," said Shirley, "my daughter Angie could come over later and keep Tom company. Then you and I could drop in for just a little while. It's Eric's farewell party. You really should go."

Eric was the paper's chief reporter, a fine newspaperman. He had landed a job with the *Los Angeles Times*. Cathy liked him a lot.

"Oh come on," said Shirley, steering Cathy to a corner of the garden. "I know how you feel about Doc. But it's been nearly 10 years. We all hope he is alive and will come home, but in the meantime you should have a life."

"You mean you want me to sleep with other men?"

"No, I'm not saying that. But it's not natural for you to isolate yourself. A little male company is good for the soul."

You'd better believe it, thought Cathy. It was something she thought about all the time, particularly at night when Tom had gone to bed. What she would give to have Doc hold her in his arms. For that matter, another man, maybe any man. She was still a young woman and very attractive. Every day she picked up eye contact from men, some of them obviously hungry for her to give even a hint of a smile …

Don't think about it, she told herself.

CHAPTER 3

The party was in full swing when Shirley and Cathy walked in.

"Hey, glad to see you," said Eric. "This is a rare honor."

"Well, I just wanted to be sure you were really going."

Eric smiled. "Well, you haven't lost your sense of humor. Look, when you get word from Doc, will you let me know?"

"Sure."

"Silence everyone." It was Donald Jones, the editor. "I have an announcement to make. We are here to say farewell to our good friend Eric, but there is another matter. Fear not, it's good news. The publisher asked me to thank you all for the success of the big travel supplement we just ran. And he has given us a gift of a free cruise for two which … which his wife obviously doesn't want to go on. Whoops, I never said that! Anyway, I am going to raffle it off right now. All your names are in the hat. Except yours, Eric!

"Okay, here we go. And the winner is Cathy!"

When the applause had died down Cathy said: "Have a redraw. I can't go."

"Yes, you can," said Donald. "You'll enjoy the trip. You don't have to go far — it's an Alaska cruise and it starts in Vancouver just 200 miles away. Take Tom with you. You can show him the state called the Last Frontier, and there's whales all the way there and back."

Cathy hurried home. Tom's light was on so she knocked on his door and went in. His bed was dwarfed by a huge picture of a Navy Crusader taking off from an aircraft carrier. Beside his bed was a picture of his father sitting in an airplane cockpit, his smile as wide as the chunky helmet he was wearing. Tom was asleep, a book cradled in his arms. Cathy took a closer look — it was a Boy Scout manual.

She froze. Tom's Boy Scout camp, she realized, was the same week as the cruise. And Donald had said the travel date could not be changed.

The next evening Cathy met Shirley in the local pub. It was a regular Thursday outing with a good bunch of regulars, although there was always one, fueled by too much ale, who would make a pass at Cathy. She did not dress to attract men, but with an hourglass figure it was hard to cover all the curves completely.

Cathy asked Shirley to come with her to Alaska. But Shirley had just started a new job and could not get away.

Then they walked back in the warm, early summer evening, the streets cheerful with a dusting of cherry blossoms. In one of the neat, little houses, most of them wood-frame cottages painted in a dozen shades of white, Cathy could see a man and a woman eating a meal. A candle burned on the table, there was a bottle of wine and a single rose in a slender vase. She looked at Shirley, who put her arm round her. "Look Cathy, I think you should go on this cruise. It will give you a chance to think things over. At the very least you can be yourself for a week. Here you're like a fish in a bowl."

CHAPTER 4
Vancouver, BC

<u>September 1982</u>

Nick Petridis leaned over the rail of the *Golden Odyssey* and looked down at Pier A of Vancouver harbor. It was 2 PM and passengers would be boarding soon. Although he was a waiter he would be busy in a few moments guiding passengers to their cabins.

He felt a hearty nudge in the ribs. "Ready for the girls?" It was his barman friend, Tony. This was the part of the job Tony really liked. For him, escorting the passengers to their cabins gave him a chance to see who was coming on board. What women, that is. And early contact was important.

Greeks are fast workers, but they didn't have to work too hard at it. Cruising had quickly acquired a romantic, if not racy, image, partly because of the television series *The Love Boat*, and more than a few passengers came aboard prepared for romantic adventures. Just the previous week, Tony had had a breathless encounter in a cabin before the ship sailed. "This is my first cruise," said a woman as he showed her in. "When does the action start?" she said with a laugh.

Tony, who thought he had seen it all, could hardly believe it when the woman shut the cabin door, lifted her cotton top to reveal two large breasts with nipples like wine corks. She pulled his head between her breasts and said, "Let's get started, big boy." What followed was fast and furious, then he made a fast exit before he was missed on deck. The rest of the week had been equally torrid, exhausting almost, but now it was another cruise and the fun would start again.

"Come on Nick," said Tony. "Find yourself a nice girl on this trip. But you'd better be quick. You know that all the good ones are accounted for before the gangway goes up."

Cathy Robertson stepped off the bus at Vancouver's cruise terminal, and found that the driver had already pulled her two bags from the hold and was hovering over them expectantly. Cathy was prepared for this and handed over $5, which the driver pocketed, wheeled around and stood by some other bags just as their owner stepped up.

Slick work, thought Cathy. But she had seen nothing yet. Next up was a porter with a trolley. He was short, fat, was sweating like a pig and smelled of stale beer. He made $100,000 a year from this job, about half of it in tax-free cash, and liked to say he gave his old lady 20 grand and spent 40 grand on beer and hookers. And the rest? "I just fritter that away."

He looked Cathy up and down like a horse at the track. "Your first cruise, ma'am?"

"Yes," said Cathy.

Excellent, thought the porter. "I'm happy to help you and I know you won't mind if I point out that we generally get $5 a bag," he lied.

Cathy knew she was being ripped off but went along with it. Heck, what's $10 when I'm getting a free cruise? But it was the same for the rest of the passengers, fare-paying or not. They were on vacation, and the porters knew it.

The porter took her to the Ocean Cruise Lines counter where an agent checked her ticket, took an imprint of her credit card and in return gave her what looked like a credit card but was a combined cabin key and ship's charge card.

That's it," said the agent. "Note your table in the dining room is 69. Your bags will go directly to your stateroom. Have a lovely cruise."

Cathy followed signs with the ship's name until she saw a gangway, then stepped aboard the *Golden Odyssey* to find a handsome young man immaculately dressed in white and holding a tray of champagne. In reality they were champagne glasses filled with sparkling wine. Behind him stood a row of equally good-looking men beaming at this woman *who was on her own*. As one they all craned their necks to look behind to make sure there was not a man in her wake.

It had to be admitted that Cathy made a pretty picture. She wore a white dress with pale blue shoes and a blue picture hat. "You look like a *Vogue* model," Shirley had said when she saw here off.

Cathy felt good about herself. She was 35 but looked 10 years younger. She ate sensibly and kept fit by walking the islands of the Olympic peninsula. She knew the cruise would be a challenge. What was the old joke about women who went to sea — you board as a passenger and you leave as freight. Cathy resolved to walk around the deck for an hour every day.

Tony was out of luck. Just as Cathy appeared he was assigned to take another passenger to her cabin. She was so overweight she looked like a large bag of potatoes tied in the middle. She was also a travel agent, and complained all the way to the cabin about not being upgraded.

"Wait till I see that swine of a sales manager who promised me a suite!" she bellowed as they disappeared down a corridor.

"Miss Robertson?" said the assistant purser to Cathy.

"Mrs. Robertson, actually."

"Oh, I see. Well — Nick will show you to your stateroom."

Nick smiled at Cathy and took her hand luggage.

"Follow me, please."

They turned off the foyer and went down a corridor lined with doors on either side.

"I see you have an outside cabin. Lucky you," said Nick. "The portholes are not big on this ship but you'll have a sea view. You might even see some dolphins or whales. Your first time to Alaska?"

"My first cruise."

"Here it is — you are on Corfu deck, cabin number 101. Sorry, I should say stateroom number 101, which is the way the cruise line prefers ..."

He was interrupted by a piercing voice from down the corridor, "and you go back to the purser and ask him where is my bottle of champagne!" It was the travel agent bellowing at Tony, who turned tail and made his escape like a rat out-running the incoming ocean.

Cathy smiled. "I suppose you get all kinds on a ship."

Nick nodded. "Your husband not on this trip?" he ventured.

"My husband ... my husband," Cathy found it hard to get the words out to a stranger. Everyone knew, but that was at home. "My husband is a pilot. He was shot down and is missing. I don't know where he is but I believe he is alive and one day we will be together again." There, she had said it, or rather blurted it out.

Nick put her bags down and his face went crimson. "I'm sorry. I did not want to intrude."

"You didn't. It's a fact and now you know."

Cathy looked out of the window and turned to Nick. He was obviously a decent man. He had an intelligent, honest face with dark eyes, attractive long eyelashes and a natural smile. "Tell me about yourself."

"I am from Corfu, just like this deck. I am a waiter because my family has a restaurant business in Greece and this is part of my training. I came on the ship last year supposedly just for one contract, which is six months, but I enjoyed it so much here I am again. The cruise industry is growing fast and I've been told I can become a head-waiter very quickly. It's not like that ashore. But I must go

… I'll look for you in the dining room. Have a good cruise."

"Thank you, Nick," said Cathy. "See you later."

"I'll look out for you tonight."

Nick rejoined the line of waiters welcoming passengers on board. Tony came over and whispered, "She's a cracker. You were gone a long time. Were you taking her clothes off?"

"She's not like that!"

"They're all like that. It's the reason they come to sea. It's romantic, they leave their inhibitions on the dock, and they drop their pants."

"Well, I think this one is different."

"Have it your own way. Hey — look at that girl!"

Their eyes swiveled to see a blonde woman in a low-cut red blouse, tight white slacks and blue shoes.

"What do you make of that?" said Tony to the waiter on his other side, figuring that Nick was a lost cause. "With those colors it looks like she has escaped from St Tropez."

"Or from the Folies Bergere," said another waiter.

"Well I saw her first," said Tony. "You guys stay clear."

CHAPTER 5
Cruising Alaska

Back in her cabin, which Cathy preferred to the word stateroom because it felt more like being at sea, she found that her garment bag was missing. Never mind, she thought, there was nothing in it she needed for the first night, so she unpacked the bags she had and found there were more than enough drawers for her things. There were two beds and she chose the one on the left because she slept on her right side and she would have a reading light over her shoulder.

Then she noticed the ice bucket on the table between the beds, and a bottle of champagne with a crisp linen towel round its neck. There was a card: "Welcome aboard — your captain."

There were also flowers, and another card. It was from her editor, Donald Jones. "Bon voyage. Have a great week and behave yourself. Your waiter probably has designs on you already."

Cathy smiled. You never know.

There was a knock on the door. "Hi, I'm your stewardess. Molly's the name. I just want to say lifeboat drill's in five minutes."

Lifeboat drill! Yikes, there was never a dull moment. In fact it was an entertaining event, for the passengers assembled in groups on the decks and heard the captain say: "Good evening. The chief officer is going to spell out the drill for emergencies. I want you all to listen carefully and follow crew instructions in the event of an emergency. Pay particular attention to the man-overboard drill — we nearly lost a passenger on the last cruise, some unwise person who was sitting on a rail. And do let us know if you see someone falling overboard ... er, even if it's someone you can't stand."

Nick looked at himself in the mirror of the tiny cabin below the waterline he shared with Tony. He was 28 but looked five years younger. He was hoping this cruise would be better than the last when the restaurant manager, an aggressive homosexual, made frequent passes at him. Many young men, particularly assistant waiters fresh from their first jobs at home, had little choice but to answer the call to his cabin. If they had said no they would have had the worst jobs to do, and perhaps be sacked.

The restaurant manager's downfall was to proposition a young man who happened to be the ship owner's son. Next thing, security officer Bill George burst into his cabin where the restaurant manager was with four young waiters. All were naked, other than the red fezzes they were wearing.

"Willies away!" said the restaurant manager, covering himself with his fez. The next day the restaurant manager was off the ship, fez and all. That's the way things happened at sea.

Nick went up to the dining room, which seated 225 passengers. There would be two seatings three times a day. The ship held 450 passengers, exactly the capacity of a Boeing 747. This was no accident — the owner built the *Golden Odyssey* this way so he could fly a planeload of passengers to the ship and fly a planeload home.

"Hi Nick," said Mike Brown, the new maître d'. Mike was a great character, an American with a Greek mother who had been with the cruise line from day one. Nick had got along with him well on the last cruise.

Nick, by this time joined by all the other waiters, was then briefed on that evening's menu. "We've got some nice fresh salmon, the lamb looks good, but of course most passengers will want a steak. Just be sure that if they ask for it well done, that they get it well done. This is a cruise ship catering to middle America and not gourmet night chez Paul Bocuse!"

As they went to their stations Mike said to Nick, "You should enjoy table 69 for the second seating — several women on their own."

Then he turned to the assembled waiters, "Okay — ready. Open the doors."

It was just 6:30 PM, but a line already stretched down the corridor to the dining room. Older passengers preferred the first sitting, and they were always on time, if not early. You could say impatient. One wore a tee shirt that said "Senior citizen — Gimme my damn discount!"

Another wore a baseball cap. The first night at sea was always casual, and this lot was typical. Too bad all the same, thought Nick. The ship's architect had designed one of the most elegant dining rooms at sea, the menus had been created by top European chefs, and his waiters were professional and looked smart.

Some of the passengers, on the other hand, were slobs. They gushed between the doors, ignoring the tuxedo-clad head waiters on either side and spread around the dining room like a rash, finding their tables and sorting themselves out boy-girl-boy-girl and so on, looking over the tables at their new friends for the next week.

The first seating went smoothly, other than one couple at a window table that had a flaming row that culminated in the wife throwing her steak, French fries and a healthy smearing of ketchup all over her husband. She then demanded to be let off the ship. As the vessel was steaming out of Vancouver's English Bay at this point, her request was badly timed.

CHAPTER 6

Cathy stood on the deck and watched the ship leave. It was a lovely evening as the *Golden Odyssey* slid backwards, was nudged around by a tug, pointed its bows at Grouse Mountain, then came around to port and lined up to pass under Lions Gate Bridge. She had read about the bridge in her guidebook. It had been built in the 1930s by a company owned by the Irish brewing family, Guinness. They owned land on the other side of the harbor, known as the North Shore, and to enable them to sell building lots they needed access. So they built this elegant bridge, which with its intricate ironwork looked quite Victorian.

As the *Golden Odyssey* went under the bridge there was a public announcement for the first seating for dinner. Cathy was in the second, at 8:30 PM. She found a deck chair and read the ship's newspaper she had found in her cabin. Tonight, it told her, was casual dress in the dining room. Fine, thought Cathy, am I to be told how to dress every night? The answer, as she would find out, was yes. On a seven-night cruise there would be two casual nights (the first and the last), two formal nights and three informal nights. The newspaper also advised that shore excursions should be selected as soon as possible. The first was in Ketchikan, a small fishing port in Alaska. She couldn't imagine the tour would be very long — twice around the totem poles might be about it. Cathy resolved to look into that.

Captain Stavros Criticos stood on the bridge of *Golden Odyssey* and let the pilot get on with the job, although he would keep a close eye on him because some years earlier a pilot put a ship on a rock just north of here. Only fast and skillful work by the captain prevented a loss of life. For the moment, though, there was time for an admiring glance at the handsome spectacle that was English Bay, where Captain Cook and then Captain Vancouver had made voyages of discovery. Spanish explorers had been here too, leaving behind many names.

"Captain," said the pilot, "as I mentioned earlier we have to lose some time because of strong tides at the Seymour Narrows. We'll turn to go up Howe Sound for a while."

Soon afterwards the vessel made a graceful turn to starboard and pointed its bows towards the snow-covered peaks of the Coast range. The ship would meander up the beautiful inlet until it got to the top and the timber mill at Woodfibre. Other than the mill there was just a dock where vessels came to load. The pilot told the captain, "You'll see a lot of bald eagles round here. You might want to tell the passengers to keep a lookout."

The dinner and "eagles about" alert came as Cathy was watching a fleet of sailing dinghies so close that she could read the name Kitsilano Yacht Club on the vessels' hulls. Several bigger yachts and powerboats came by and on one flying bridge a young man blew a kiss. For me? Cathy smiled anyway, then turned and headed below.

Mike Brown looked quite debonair, as always, as he welcomed his guests to dinner. He saw them as guests and the cruise line referred to them as such, but Jack Silver, the travel writer who was on board, would have disagreed. Guests did not pay; the people on board had paid plenty and were passengers. Mike, however, had a flourish to him that made everyone feel like, well, a guest. He took Cathy by the arm and led her to a table on the right. It was for eight, and all the other passengers were already seated. Jack Silver stood up and said, "Hi. I've already met the others so let me introduce them."

There was Ruby, whom Cathy immediately recognized as the pushy travel agent she had met when she boarded.

Flo was quite elderly, and almost deaf.

Ivan and Christine looked interesting. They were beautifully, and formally dressed, Christine in an elegant dress and Ivan in a well-cut suit and silk tie, Hermes by the look of it. The dress code in the ship's newspaper had said the first night was casual, but everyone would learn that this was as casual as Ivan ever appeared in public.

Then there were May and June, mother and daughter who looked more like sisters. They wore simple but revealing clothes. The passengers, and the crew, would be seeing a lot more of them, literally, as the cruise went on.

The introductions over, Cathy sat down. At the same moment Nick appeared as if from nowhere and spread her starched linen napkin on her lap.

"Good evening, madam," said Nick. "Here is tonight's menu."

"Hi Nick. We meet again," she smiled.

"You'll meet him every night for the next week," said Ruby. "Hey Nick — what's special for tonight?"

"It's all on the menu, madam."

"In that case I'll start with the prawn cocktail, gimme a green salad and then the sirloin steak well done."

Nick worked his way round the table until he got to Ivan.

"Caviar, please."

"Hey, that's not on the menu," exclaimed Ruby.

"No harm in asking," said Ivan.

Nick held up his hands. "I'll see what I can do." He would have to talk to Mike Brown.

Ruby was about to open her mouth again when the sommelier arrived. He wore a red jacket with a silver cup around his neck. This was the badge of office of the man in charge of the wine, Marco being his name.

"Ladies and gentlemen," said Marco with a flourish. "As you probably know, your wines are included at no extra charge. Of course we have other wines that you might want to consider for a special occasion, such as being alive (and here Flo gave him a little wave) and for these you have to pay. But tonight we have a nice little

Australian chardonnay, and to follow a red merlot from Chile."

Turning to Flo, he bent down to her ear and said: "Your usual champagne, madam?"

Flo nodded and smiled to the table, "I can recommend a glass of champagne every night of your life. Keeps you young, although it doesn't do much for the hearing. As it's the start of the cruise, I'd like to buy you all a glass."

A murmur of approval went around the table. When Jack's glass was filled he offered a toast to Flo and she replied, "I love to be at sea. It beats an old folks' home if you can afford it."

At that moment there was a slight shudder as the *Golden Odyssey* reached the top of the narrow inlet and reversed one engine to make a turn. On shore there was just a sawmill and a few houses in the tiny community called Woodfibre, as well as a loading dock for large ships. But it was brightly lit. So well lit in fact, that it could have been Las Vegas-by-the-sea.

Christine, who was sitting by a porthole, took a look and said to Nick, "Tell me, what's the name of that city out there?"

"That city," said Nick, without missing a beat, "is called Woodfibre, madam."

Then Ivan's caviar arrived, along with the trimmings of blinis, chopped egg and onions. He beamed at Christine as he picked up his fork.

Ruby just glared.

This, thought Jack, is going to be an interesting cruise.

CHAPTER 7

The first night of a cruise is never the liveliest because many passengers are tired after a long day getting to the ship. The crew has also been working flat out to dispatch the last group of passengers, clean the cabins, and indeed the entire vessel, load provisions, welcome the next group of passengers and get all the bags to the right cabins. Just to complicate matters there are often visits while the ship is in port, usually groups of travel agents. They are given a tour of the ship, lunch and a sales pitch by the cruise line's local sales manager. Nick had worked that day's lunch in Vancouver. He would rather have rented a bike and gone for a ride around Stanley Park — but next time.

Cathy and Jack left the dining room together. Nick was at the door with Mike Brown who bowed and said: "Hope you enjoyed your dinner. Have a good evening."

"Crew bar for you tonight?" said Jack to Nick.

"No way," said Nick, "we've just been told some bags are missing so I have to go and try to sort them out."

Cathy said, "I think one of them might be mine — a black garment bag?"

"I'll take a look and bring it to your cabin," said Nick.

Jack scooped a handful of mints from a dish as they left the dining room and walked along a corridor lined with paintings. "See this stuff?" said Jack. "In a day or two there will be an art auction. You'd be surprised at the quality of the artwork and how many sales are made. As for the buyers, it takes all kinds and I've heard that a big seller is Elvis on velvet."

Cathy laughed. "You seem to know your way around. This is not your first cruise then?"

"No way! I'm a travel writer and I've been on more than 100 ships, and I've seen some terrible things hanging on walls. One ship had a corridor with pictures of ships in storms. You know — blue water, white spray and waves the size of houses lashing little boats. Some people would get seasick just walking by them."

Then they were in the casino. "Bit noisy in here," said Jack, "but we have to walk through it to get to the bar. The casino is here so that when you want to go anywhere else you have to go through it. As you can imagine, the cruise line gets a cut of the take and that's why it's open morning, noon and night, although not when the ship is in port. Here, turn right — this is a nice little bar."

Cathy and Jack walked in to find a room with tables, a bar with seats and a small dance floor. A combo was playing but nobody was dancing. "First night blues," said Jack. "Just wait till tomorrow night — this place will be jumping. Anyway, what would you like?"

"Good question — what do old sea dogs have for a nightcap?"

"A wee whisky was what my old Scottish mother thrived on."

"Done."

Jack led Cathy to the bar and said, "Two small Famous Grouse please, each with three large pieces of ice and still water on the side. Got Evian?"

"Certainly sir. Two Low Flyers coming up," said the barman.

Jack took Cathy to a table at the back. "We'll sit here. The barman will bring the drinks over. Now, tell me about yourself. What's a nice girl like you doing in a place like this?"

The drinks came, they made a toast to a good cruise, and Cathy told her story. Everything, but first she made him promise not to write about her.

"Wow, quite a yarn! Too bad I'm sworn to secrecy," said Jack when Cathy had finished. "I hope you find your husband one day, and soon."

"Well, thank you for being a good listener."

Cathy sipped her drink, then put her hand on Jack's arm. "I gather that some women run away to sea, as they say, to have a wild time. I won't be doing that."

"No, I don't suppose you will. But if on the other hand you do meet someone whose company you enjoy then don't forget you're only on the *Golden Odyssey* for a week, not for life."

Cathy smoothed her skirt, looked at Jack and said, "What about you?"

"Me? I'm gay."

"Oh ..."

"Surprised? I'm glad. Actually I'm just kidding, but I love Woody Allen's line about the advantage of being bisexual — it doubles your chance of a date on Saturday night. But I have a girlfriend, so you're safe, Cathy, for now!"

Cathy liked this man. He was tall, good-looking, dressed in a dark suit with a black open-necked shirt, with ebony hair flopping over one eye. But there was nothing dark about his style. He moved languidly, smiled easily and had a warm sense of humor. And a travel writer? That sounded interesting. She looked forward to spending more time with him, but not tonight.

"I'll leave you to sort out your sex life. Time I went to bed and gathered together my luggage."

CHAPTER 8

Cathy walked to the door of the bar and hesitated, wondering which way to her cabin. At that very moment an officer came by.

"Excuse me," said Cathy. "How do I get to C101?"

"Aha," said the officer. "I am the captain so I should know something about finding places. Let me tell you something very useful. Cabins on the starboard side have odd numbers, and on the port side even numbers. So you are on the correct side of the ship. One other thing – you might not know if you are going to the front or the back, which we call forward or aft. All you have to do is look down – see the whale pattern on the carpet? The whales are swimming to towards the bows of the ship. Simple, eh."

Cathy thought about this and said, "Of course I could always look out of a window to see which way we are going, or heaven forbid, go out on deck."

"You could, and can I recommend you do that right now, because it is a beautiful evening and my pilot has everything under control." With that Captain Criticos waved Cathy to a nearby door and opened it for her.

They stepped outside on to a deck washed by a full moon...

The land that she knew was Canada seemed incredibly close. "This part of British Columbia is among the fairest I have seen in all my years at sea," said the captain.

"And you, my girl," and at this he slipped his arm around her waist, "are fairer still."

Cathy froze. It was the first time in years that a man had been this close.

The captain's grip tightened, but Cathy turned to face him. "Captain," said Cathy with a mockingly wary smile, "I hardly know you."

"Don't worry, I don't try to seduce passengers on the deck. You know we have security cameras everywhere and my officers on the bridge can probably see us now. I don't want to get them too excited."

"Well I'm glad to hear that," said Cathy. "I wouldn't like a film of our meeting to turn up in the crew bar."

The captain laughed. "My company would be upset. And so would my wife and eight children."

"Eight children! I assume they let you go home now and again."

"Yes, I get very good leave, which reminds me the reason I get to be on deck right now is because I am training a relief captain. He is actually very experienced but he has to get to know this part of the coast they call the Inside Passage."

"So why are you not on the bridge with him now?"

"Because we have a pilot and he is an excellent man who can teach my colleague the position of every rock. These are tricky waters, narrow with fast currents, such as the Seymour Narrows we just went through."

"I missed that," said Cathy.

"There used to be a huge rock in the middle of the channel that had sunk many ships. But a few years ago the Canadian government had it blown up by engineers who made a tunnel and packed it with explosives. At the time it was the biggest ever non-nuclear explosion, and it did the job. But even with the rock gone we have to take care, and make sure no other ships are transiting the narrows at the same time.

"Look out for the Seymour Narrows on the return passage. It fact you are welcome to come to the bridge and I'll show you the location on a chart. But now I have to get back there. Good night and see you tomorrow evening for my Welcome Aboard party."

"Yes, see you then — good night." Cathy watched the captain stride along the deck. He was straight out of a cruise line brochure, tall and so handsome in his white uniform. Oh my God, she almost said out loud. How he looked like Doc. She reached in her bag for a handkerchief to wipe her eyes. As she did so the ship keeled over ever so slightly as it negotiated a channel. She saw a mountain rising steeply from the water's edge like the walls of a fjord. The moonlight showed everything almost like daylight — many rocks with wash from the ship breaking over them, and pieces of wood she knew would be tree trunks that had escaped from log booms. Coming from Seattle she knew all about logging.

She thought about Tom. Must call him at the first port. But he's at a Boy Scout camp in a field, and how could he take a call? Hey, kid, she said to herself, pull yourself together. You're on holiday. Okay, a man has just made a pass at you, but that is not all bad.

CHAPTER 9

Cathy stepped over the doorsill and on to the carpet, noted the whales swimming to the right, and went with the flow. First thing she saw was a big sign for an art auction the next day. She laughed to herself when she thought of passengers bidding for Elvis on velvet, then carried on through the casino with its jingling bells from fruit machines, dodged a group of dice players who tried to rope her in for a roll — "bring us some luck, honey" — and made it out, down wide stairs that could have come from Tara Hall, and sure enough there was her cabin, C101. Whew, ruminated Cathy, not many dull moments so far.

She was just putting her key in the door when a voice said, "Allow me."

It was Nick, and he had her garment bag.

"Sorry it's so late. Some bags did not get to the ship until we were just about to leave and there was no time to get them to the passengers before dinner. I hope it was not too much of an inconvenience for you?"

"Not at all. I had been warned to take essentials in a carry-on bag. But I'm sure ready for a shower now, and then bed. By the way, I've been told the crew members are the best people to talk to about shore excursions. I mean, you guys have been here lots of times and I suppose you know where to find the best shops — Bloomingdales, Hermes and so on."

Nick smiled, "Ketchikan awaits your shopping pleasure if you are looking for the very best fishing tackle. I have to say that the ship's excursion is not expensive but if you're adventurous you can do your own thing. It's nice, too, to step off as a free agent and go where you please."

"Couldn't agree more," said Cathy. "Now, if you'll just put my bags here, I'll say goodnight."

Nick brought the bags into the cabin, gave a little bow, and said, "Lovely to have you on board."

Cathy saw just a sensation of hesitation as Nick stepped to the doorway. She started to say "good night" but her mouth moved to softly blow a kiss.

The door closed and Cathy was left wondering what had happened. Why had she done that? She felt her heart beating quickly. Cathy girl, she admonished herself, you had better keep a firm grip on yourself. The vessel has barely left the dock and you've had an encounter with the captain, and now another man is making you feel like a giddy young girl.

Cathy took a photo from her bag and put it on the table beside the bed. It showed Doc and her when they first met. She was a young girl then. As she gazed at the photo her mind raced through the stages of her life, from those days to the time they were married, to motherhood, Doc's disappearance, and today. Years had passed, but tonight she did not feel any older, any less of a young girl. Was it being on the ship, suddenly in a different world, that gave her this feeling?

She got undressed and turned out the light.

In the cabin next door, May and her daughter June had also taken their clothes off, although sleep was far from their minds. May was in bed with one of the ship's photographers, a boy called Mark who was less than half her age, while June was in the bed opposite with a waiter who had been a complete stranger until he arrived with a sandwich five minutes earlier. This was room service with a difference.

"You ladies always operate like this?" asked the waiter, whose name was George and who might have been 20 but handled the situation as if this happened every night. Maybe it did.

"Well," said May, "I am June's mother and we have our own way of doing things. We hit the bars earlier but being the first night everyone is unpacking or asleep and it was dead out there. But then we met Mark and he's a lovely fellow — aren't you Mark?" said May, her hand running down his naked belly. Mark's body shuddered.

George looked at his watch. He was working and would be missed if he stayed too long. And so he pulled up the sheet, rolled June on her back, and got on with it.

The things I do for Greece, thought George.

CHAPTER 10

The next morning was perfect in the Inside Passage. Up on the bridge, the pilot nursed a mug of coffee, had the other hand on a pair of binoculars, and checked the chart one more time. The *Golden Odyssey* was coming out of a long channel. Now the vessel had to go to starboard, round an island, then back to port. On the pilot's order the helmsman put the wheel over 10 degrees and the ship responded smartly. The pilot enjoyed being on a small ship that moved like a speedboat compared to his last charge, which was a 200,000-ton oil tanker. It took miles to turn and even more miles to stop. The money had been good but this job was better. Vancouver-based pilots were never away from home for long and he would be getting off at Prince Rupert where an American pilot would take over.

Another bend in the channel and dead ahead was a small boat. The pilot picked up his binoculars and took a look — there was just one person on board and he or she was busy with a fish. It looked like a big one the way the rod was bending. The question was, however, could he get the ship between the side of the fjord and the boat in question? He decided it was not a good idea to try and asked the helmsman to sound the ship's whistle.

This startled the fisherman, who looked around to see a very large ship bearing down on him. He hesitated for a moment, shook his head, then his fist, and putting his rod into a holder on the deck, applied power gently in the hope of getting out of the way, and keeping the fish. It was not to be. The fish, probably not unaware of the presence of *Golden Odyssey*, made a dive, the rod bent in a dramatic fashion, and then the line broke. Zing! The rod straightened up, kept going and smacked the hapless fisherman on the back.

The pilot went to the platform on the side of the bridge known as the wing as the ship went by the fishing boat. He held out his hands as a gesture that said, "what could he do?". The fisherman shook his fist again and shouted something that was lost in the wind. Just as well.

Cathy woke as the ship heeled ever so slightly in its first turn. She got out of bed and picked up the papers that had been pushed under her cabin door. One was a U.S.-produced newspaper, sent by fax and photocopied on the ship. The other was the ship's daily program. This she wanted to see. Okay, thought Cathy, what's on today? She knew the ship was at sea all day — well, in the Inside Passage. There was an aerobics class at 9 AM. That was in 30 minutes. She dressed quickly, went to the café at *Golden Odyssey*'s stern, and helped herself to a yoghurt and cereal. Cathy looked around for somewhere to sit, then noticed tables on the open deck. She went outside but they were all taken. Then she saw Flo by herself.

"Can I join you?" asked Cathy.

Flo looked up and smiled. "Of course, sit down. Looks like you are dressed for the gym."

"Yes," said Cathy, "I want to enjoy the food on board but I think I'd better get some exercise as well."

"Good idea, my dear," said Flo. "We never did that sort of thing in my day, but the world has changed. What do you call these exercises — aeronautics?"

Later, Cathy walked to the health club and saw Ruby just ahead of her, and then May and June. Good heavens — Jack was there too.

"I tell you," said Jack by way of greeting, "I simply hate these damn gyms but what else can you do? I like to eat and I love to drink, and something has to give. This!" he said with a wide smile, pinching a roll of flesh from his waist.

Then they were in session, being led by a trim gentle-man called Richard. He would not see 60 again, but looked 10 years younger. Richard's main job on board was as a dance host, which meant he was to socialize with women traveling on their own. However, he had been a gymnastics instructor in the army and had a very fit, lean frame. Cruise director John Dean took one look and gave him the job. "You mean in addition to dancing and doing shore excursions as well?"

"Richard — that's cruising. Everyone has to double up."

So Richard led the aerobics class, and very popular he was too. He didn't work the passengers too hard, which suited most of them, sending them away with a mild sweat and the feeling they had done something.

"You know what?" said Jack to Cathy as they left. "That was a nice little loosener-upper. But the thing that really works for me is walking round the deck. That I like to do after lunch."

"I'll join you if I may," said Cathy. "I like to walk but don't have the resolve to go far on my own."

"You're right. I find talking to someone makes the miles pass and I never notice the pain. See you at reception at 4 PM and we'll go down to the promenade deck."

"You're on," said Cathy.

Jack disappeared to his cabin to do some writing and Cathy sought out the main deck bar where she had spied an Italian coffee machine.

"Coffee please," she asked the barman.

"Black or white," said Tony.

"Well black of course, the way they do it in Italy."

"No problem. I just thought that with you being American …"

"We don't all drink that dishwater stuff," said Cathy with a smile. "I like real coffee and have a machine at home where I grind my own beans."

"To be honest," said Tony, "I'm not an expert in coffee. I'm not even a very good barman, but the regular barman fell and broke his arm and I'm taking his place. In fact I had been waiting for an opportunity to train as a barman and this might be it."

"Well too bad about the other guy, but I hope you do well."

Tony served Cathy's coffee and looked her up and down with a practiced eye. A real beauty, he thought, but not the eager type, not like the blonde he saw the previous day.

Then there she was. And she came to the bar.

Her name was Diane and she was from Florida, where she and her husband had a chain of fashion shops. One of them had to be there all the time so they took separate vacations. Her husband went off playing golf with his buddies and she went cruising. Diane took one look at Tony — young, handsome and with a racy look in his eye — and decided he was her man.

"Got a good eye-opener?" she said to Tony.

Tony looked at Diane. She was late thirties, wearing a tight, short skirt, a figure-hugging low-cut blouse and looked full of promise.

"Anything you'd like to open, I've got it right here," ventured Tony with a trace of a wicked grin.

"Well," said Diane, reaching into her bag for a cigarette, "I'll start with a drink. What about a gin and tonic, but easy on the tonic."

"Coming right up."

Cathy excused herself and headed back to her cabin thinking ... that's how it's done.

CHAPTER 11

At lunchtime she went back to the stern café. She decided that being outside was the place to be as the weather was good and the scenery absorbing.

First person she met was Nick. "Isn't this beautiful," she said, as the ship went by a small island with a fine stand of fir trees.

"Look — there's an eagle over there. See — the tree on the right," said Nick.

Several passengers went over to the ship's rail and passed round a pair of binoculars.

"What a handsome fellow," said Cathy. "You know it might be America's national bird but you hardly ever see them down our way. I've heard there are lots here."

"Yes," said Nick. There's a place called Squamish on the road between Vancouver and Whistler where at certain times of the year scores of them gather. But you'll see plenty on this cruise. Do you have binoculars?"

"No, but I think I'll look for some in Ketchikan. I don't want to miss a thing on this trip."

Cathy went to her table and Nick brought a menu. "Have you decided what you are doing in Ketchikan?"

"There is a shore excursion but I think I'll just go for a stroll."

"I know a shop where you can get binoculars at a good price. One of the crew bought a pair on the last trip. They were quite cheap and work very well."

Then Nick added, hesitantly, "I'll have the morning off and I'm also going to have a walk in Ketchikan. I know a nice place with a view for a coffee. I can show you where this shop is."

Cathy did not hesitate. "Good idea. What time?"

"Well the ship docks at 7 in the morning, and it will be cleared by 8. You need breakfast, I have to serve it and tidy up. Let's meet at the bottom of the gangway at 9.30?"

"Done," said Cathy.

The rest of the day seemed to pass in a flash. Cathy met Jack on the deck and they walked for an hour. They walked clockwise around the deck although Jack warned her that they might be doing the wrong thing. The what? Well, said Jack, there was a right way and a wrong way to do most things at sea, but he was darned if he could re-member if clockwise was correct.

Lo and behold they came across Ivan and Christine walking in the opposite direction.

"Good afternoon," said Ivan, lifting a battered Panama hat. "Lovely day for a dander."

"Yes indeed, "said Jack effusively, "See you next time around."

Cathy said hello as well and turned to Jack, "Well one of us, or should I say two of us, will be right."

"It's us. It's a process of elimination. I'm going to be very arrogant and say that because that pair can't be right because I can't be wrong."

"As you wish," said Cathy. Men!

Dinner was a rather grand affair with most passengers making an effort. For men it was just a matter of shaking the mothballs out of their tuxedos, while several women had fallen for sequin tops and long black skirts. Cathy wore a simple white, linen blouse and Thai silk skirt that came to her ankles. She stood in front of the mirror in her cabin and reached into a small bag, taking out a simple gold bracelet. It had a charm as well, a little gold airplane. It had been a present from Doc to mark their first wedding anniversary and his qualifying as a Navy pilot. She held it to her heart for a moment, then quickly put it on. "Well Doc," she said trying her best to smile. "You and I are going out tonight. Take care of me."

The meal was a fun gathering with Jack in fine form. "Did you go ashore today?" he asked June.

"Huh?" said June "Did we stop today? Did I miss something?"

"No darling," said her mother, "You did not miss much, although you did not venture far beyond your cabin."

June blushed at the thought. She had stayed in bed all morning and then called room service for lunch. She made a point of asking for George to deliver lunch, saying he had left his pen in the cabin when he had made the previous night's delivery. George brought the lunch, was hauled into bed, and had to explain himself again when he got back to the galley.

Marco the wine steward came by and poured wine for the table. Ivan and Christine had a bottle of Chateau Beychevelle, Flo had her usual champagne, and the others had the house wine. Everyone said cheers and clinked glasses. It was clear that Ruby would rather have had the good Bordeaux or the champagne.

But the meal was a success and Cathy waved to Nick as she left. "See you tomorrow," she said, Nick's smile sending her away with a warm glow. I could get to like this man, she thought.

CHAPTER 12

"Ladies and gentlemen," said John Dean, the cruise director. "Welcome to the ballroom. Tonight it is my pleasure to present the master of the *Golden Odyssey*, Captain Stavros Criticos!"

There was a generous round of applause and thousands of sequins quivered.

In public, the captain was a man of few words so he wasted little time introducing his senior officers. "Now you know who they are, if you have any complaints, these are the people to talk to. If you have any compliments, please come and tell me."

Cathy was standing with Jack and Richard, the dance host. When the music started and couples began to dance Richard turned to Cathy and said, "Please excuse me, but I'm on duty now. I would love to dance with you but my job description rules out my consorting with anyone so attractive."

With a gallant bow Richard backed off and headed for an elderly widow who had been watching them with an impatient look. He would tell Cathy later that this was one of the toughest jobs at sea. The single women on board who wished to avail themselves of the dance hosts' attention had worked out how many dances each should have. Woe betide Richard if he favored one woman over the others. His boss, the cruise director, would probably not notice — but the women would.

Cathy returned to her cabin, opened the cruise line's folder on a table, and took out writing paper and an envelope. If they were going to be in port tomorrow this was a good time to write to Doc. It was not easy writing to someone who never replied, so she went to the porthole and looked out at the night sky for inspiration.

Where are you? she asked a full moon skidding between light clouds. *Well, wherever you are I want you to know I am here and thinking about you. Tonight I am on a stout ship taking me to an adventure in Alaska. This is a trip you would enjoy. Tell you what, let's say I am checking it out for you ...*

Cathy turned back to the table and sat down. Her thoughts went on to the paper quickly now, which was just as well as something was going on next door. Ah yes, May and June's cabin. They were entertaining again. I wonder, thought Cathy, if they know how thin these walls are. It reminded her of a friend's experience at an airport hotel in Frankfurt. As he had told Cathy, "I could hear *everything* even without putting a glass to the wall."

She got into bed with a smile, and slept the sleep of the good.

CHAPTER 13

Ketchikan greeted the *Golden Odyssey* with a curtain of cloud. Cathy stood on deck and took in the little town and its harbor. The sea was calm, a light drizzle fell, and seagulls wheeled over a fishing boat that was unloading its catch.

Jack Silver came by.

"Hi Jack, I'm just wondering if we'll get the catch of the day at dinner tonight."

Jack nodded towards the fishing boat, put his hand on Cathy's shoulder, and said, "I hate to disillusion you, but tonight's dinner is in the freezer. So are tomorrow's lunch and dinner, and the next day's. We will eat from the freezer until the ship returns to Vancouver and loads a container from Los Angeles.

"You want to eat fresh food? Go ashore for lunch, which I heartily recommend. That way you will get crab fresh as fresh can be, and very likely at a dockside restaurant with lots of atmosphere. Otherwise take a smaller ship, which has a chef who has the time to go shopping in local markets. But that will cost bigger bucks than you are paying for this cruise.

"I'll never forget," said Jack, warming to the topic, "being on a ship somewhere in the South China Sea. At dinner one night the menu said *fresh Lake Michigan trout*. I said to the waiter 'we're were a long way from Lake Michigan so what's this fiction about it being fresh?'

"You know what the waiter told me? He said, 'well sir, it was fresh when it was caught!'

"The best you can hope for is that it went straight on to ice, and the term for that is *fresh frozen*."

Cathy put her hand on Jack's arm and said she would think of him every time she had fish. Jack laughed and went on his way.

Which left Cathy at the railing thinking this was getting better by the day. Here she was making new friends quickly and comfortably, and there was no doubt it was because she was on a ship. That would not happen in a hotel. No way, she thought. People don't talk to one another in hotels. What was the old saying — all being in the same boat?

"Morning Cathy," said a cheery voice.

It was Ivan. "Going ashore?"

"You bet," said Cathy. "I might just buy a pair of binoculars so I can see the icebergs coming. You know what happened to the Titanic."

Ivan laughed and hurried on his way, presumably to tell Christine the ship had docked.

Cathy was on the dock at 9:25. It was a lovely morning with a clear sky. But there was a bit of a breeze coming off the sea, as she could see from the seagulls soaring effortlessly overhead. The sudden roar of an engine made her look around to see a small floatplane start its takeoff run across the rippled sea.

Then she saw Nick.

"Ready to roll?" he said as he stepped on to the dock.

"Lead on MacDuff," said Cathy.

They walked off the dock and crossed the street to a row of shops. The first sold clothing for the outdoors, the second fishing tackle, and the third was a bank.

"As I said, everything for the modern woman, but at least there's a bank."

Cathy laughed. "It doesn't bother me. I'm not a shopper. What about a coffee?"

"I know just the place," said Nick, and with that he took her hand and wheeled her round back towards the harbor.

The gesture was more guidance that affection, and Cathy understood that. But it felt good all the same. She had a friend.

CHAPTER 14

They strolled along a sidewalk with the sea on their left. There were more fishing boats, a dock with several float-planes, and beyond a ferry arriving from Juneau up the coast. What they saw was a little town at work, a no-nonsense place where most men fished, hunted and drank beer. They drove pickup trucks and had big dogs that rode in the back. Their humor ran to putting ads on bar room walls saying they wanted to meet a woman with a boat and a motor — "please send photo of the boat and motor."

Cathy was just happy to be ashore. The cruise was fine but it was a chance to see somewhere new. Soon enough they got to a coffee shop. They went in and sat by the window. The walls were decorated with fishing nets and bits of driftwood.

"This is quite nice, actually," said Cathy. "I think I pre-fer this décor to some of the rooms on the ship, particular-ly those with the awful pictures for sale. I think the art auctioneer must be more of a salesman than an art lover."

They ordered their coffee and Nick nodded in agreement. "He's a salesman all right — probably a car salesman by trade. I don't know if you noticed but the ship's newspaper had a promotion today for an art auction and it said our man had *new works from old masters!*"

Cathy laughed and Nick continued, "I asked the art auctioneer about that on the last cruise and he told me some of the old masters are still alive. But if you ask me, the artists are old rather than masters."

The coffee arrived and Cathy looked out of the window. "You know this is probably quite a nice little town. Too small for me though. I like where I am. It's big enough so that there are good jobs, places to go and some cultural life."

"When I'm traveling and get to a place," said Nick, "I always wonder if I can live there. Don't get me wrong — I'm not unhappy with my home and I'm not a nomad, but it's an automatic reaction to look around and see what appeal a place has."

Cathy looked him in the eye. "Are you looking for paradise?"

"I've not been at sea all that long but I have seen a lot of the world and I have not found a place that is perfect. I don't think paradise exists."

"Does anywhere come close?"

"I don't know. I think it will be a decision I will make with a lover."

"You are a romantic, Nick," said Cathy.

"Yes, I suppose I am."

With that he blushed. Cathy put her hand on his and said, "I'll help you look — well, as a friend, if that's okay."

"I'd like that," sad Nick. Then, gathering himself, he went on, "now what about a stroll back to the ship? Unless, that is, you'd like to see any of the town attractions. Let's see, where will we start — what about the recycling depot?"

CHAPTER 15

That evening *Golden Odyssey* slipped away from the dock at Ketchikan and resumed its voyage up the Inside Passage to Skagway. Captain Criticos stood on the bridge with the pilot who would guide the vessel in American waters, he took in the dramatic scenery of sea and mountains, and felt satisfied. All was well with his beautiful ship.

Below decks, Tony checked his tie in the mirror of his cabin and looked at his watch. He was on duty in 20 minutes, just enough time to see if Diane had moved to her new cabin.

Crew, such as barmen, were not allowed in passenger accommodation areas, but there were ways to get into cabins with almost no risk. Tony knew when the ship sailed that a prime cabin was empty because of a plumbing problem. Now it was fully functioning, he had a friend in the purser's office, and his plan was unfolding.

Diane's new cabin was right across from a crew service area. Tony loved that — very apt.

In other words Tony could make his way through the innards of the ship, open the crew service door into the passenger corridor — and there was Diane's cabin right opposite. Maybe four feet away.

Tony picked up a phone and called the cabin number.

"Hello." It was Diane.

"Hi — it's me, Tony. How do you like your cabin?"

"Wonderful. It's much bigger than the one I had. Also I have a lovely big window instead of a porthole. I can't thank you enough. I must say I like a man who gets things done."

You're seen nothing yet, thought Tony.

"It's a pleasure," he purred. "Can I take a look?"

"But of course."

"I'll be right up. One thing — they have funny rules on the ship about where crew can go. Can you open the door just a little bit and I'll come over from the door opposite."

"Sure," said Diane, enjoying the intrigue.

Tony knew there was something else — a big bed, replacing the two singles she had before.

He walked quickly through the crowded crew areas, took a service lift up four decks, walked down a corridor with a metal floor and bare walls, then came to a door with a large sign: YOU ARE ENTERING A PASSENGER AREA. SMILE! He looked around, quickly opened the door, and saw carpet and opposite a cabin door, B936, and it was slightly ajar.

He checked behind himself one more time, put his head into the corridor, which was also clear, then hurried to the other side, pushing open the cabin door.

"Well, fancy meeting you here," said a delighted Diane. "I can't thank you enough for moving me to this rather swish cabin."

"It's a pleasure. But I can't linger as I'm about to go on duty. I just wanted to check that everything was all right. Anything you need?"

"Well, yes, but you have to work," said Diane mischievously. "Tell you what — maybe you can drop by this very nice cabin when you close the bar tonight."

"I'd like that," said Tony, kissing her gently on the cheek. Then he put his finger to her lips, wheeled around, checked the corridor via the door spy-hole, and then he was gone. Just like the Scarlet Pimpernel.

CHAPTER 16

Dawn was breaking as *Golden Odyssey* arrived at Skagway, gateway to the Klondike, where gold was discovered in 1896 by George Carmack and Skookum Jim. It started a stampede of 100,000 would-be prospectors to Bonanza and Eldorado creeks, although fewer than 40,000 were able to make the arduous journey through the mountain passes into Canada's Yukon Territory.

In 1897 two ships arrived in San Francisco with gold worth more than $1 billion in today's money, but it was Seattle that became the supply center. Gold fever was so high here that the stampede was joined by the mayor, 12 policemen and many of the city's streetcar drivers.

Skagway soon rivaled San Francisco for hotels and banks. Miners needed a large quantity of stores to get to the diggings and here everything was on sale, such as packhorses for up to $700, almost $20,000 in today's money. Miners were also robbed by saloonkeepers and dance hall girls, and scores never made it out of town.

Today Skagway lives on its memories, making it a popular stop for cruise ship passengers. Some had drinks at a surviving gold rush saloon and visited the forlorn cemetery where gunfighters lie six feet under. Cathy was tempted by the White Pass & Yukon Route railway excursion on a spectacular line dating back to 1898, but could not imagine doing it without her son Tom. So, next time.

She joined Nick and they went to the bar where it was standing room only, then Nick spotted Tony at a table. Then pushed their way through the crowd and saw there were two seats. "Can we sit here?" said Nick.

"Sure, join the party," said Tony. "Meet my friend Diane."

The others at the table were not all strangers. There was May and June, along with two young crewmen, and just coming over was Jack Silver.

"Hi Jack," said Cathy. "Fancy meeting you here."

"I tell you, my friend, on this cruise there are two bars where everyone goes. The next one is at Juneau and we'll all be there as well. There ain't a lot of culture on this trip but you do get to have a few beers."

"Is that all?" said Diane into Tony's ear. "He's not having as much fun as we are," and she laughed a little too loudly. Nick looked over at Tony, who rolled his eyeballs. Red they were too, souvenirs of a torrid night just passed, when he had sneaked back to Diane's room, found her standing tall in a silk negligee. Tony had been everything she was looking for — young, strong and a practiced lover, who left her with a smile on her face and one word on her lips — *more!*

Cathy guessed that Tony and Diane had something going. Good luck to them, she thought. She was beginning to see the cruise as a microcosm of life in which lots of people were thrown together in a small space, living their lives, but at a faster pace because they just had a week. And they were on a ship, which seemed to put them into overdrive.

She was far away with her thoughts when she felt a hand on her leg. It was Nick, giving her a playful squeeze.

"You okay? You seem far away."

"I was. The noise in here put my mind into neutral and I was daydreaming."

"Mind if we go now — I have to get back to the ship to prepare for a deck BBQ tonight."

CHAPTER 17

And so it went on. Some passengers on the *Golden Odyssey* did little more than learn the finer points of bingo, and not a few struggled to understand the language of the sea — fore and aft, port and starboard, etc. One woman asked if the crew slept on board, another wanted to know the time of the midnight buffet. But as the days went by and lives were lived, a community of sorts developed. People talked to one another easily, friendships were made, and love affairs developed.

And Cathy was not immune.

It happened when *Golden Odyssey* slipped into Glacier Bay. It was a perfect morning — cold as you'd expect, but sunny too, so that the passengers on the deck did not know what to wear. Some were in fur coats, others in bikinis.

Cathy stood on deck near the bows as Captain Criticos took the vessel ever so slowly towards a wall of ice. As it inched closer she could see it was perhaps 50 feet high, brilliantly white with currents of blue running through it.

The sea below was a muddy color from the pieces of ice that had fallen into the water — calving, a Parks Service ranger called it in her commentary.

A hundred yards or so from the glacier the ship stopped. Passengers crowded the decks with binoculars and cameras.

Cathy couldn't see anyone she knew but didn't care. This was a natural wonder and she was there. Then she heard a ripping sound, followed by a loud crack, and there was a murmur of excitement from the watching passengers as a huge piece of ice separated from the glacier and started to fall into the bay.

Instinctively she stepped back a little, then realized there was someone behind her. It was Nick. His hands were on her waist and when they squeezed gently, she turned her head and she had to stop herself from kissing him.

"Hello Nick. I could get used to that."

CHAPTER 18

Golden Odyssey carried on to Juneau where half the passengers, certainly many of the crew, crowded into the Red
Dog saloon, famous for its sawdust floor and Wyatt
Earp's six-shooter. He had checked it in at the bar one
night, but when he went to claim it the next morning, pri-
or to getting on an early steamer, he found the bar safe
was still locked.

Other passengers, including Cathy, walked along the
Juneau waterfront and boarded floatplanes for flights
over the glaciers. Jack had to use all his charm to get
Cathy to sign up for this excursion. "It is the highlight of
the cruise. Don't miss it."

Cathy argued it was an icing on the cake, and that going without Tom — and indeed Doc — would be a selfish
indulgence. "Look," said Jack, "this excursion is so good
you will want to do it again. And Tom will be impressed
at your taking a ride in a small plane."

And so she sat in the co-pilot seat of the six-passenger
Beaver and strapped herself in. "Okay," said the pilot, a

guy in shorts who looked barely older than Tom. "Your lifejackets are under your seats, and no smoking in rows 32 to 48." With that he opened the cockpit door and pushed the plane away from the dock with his foot. The cockpit door closed, he turned to Cathy and said with a smile, "This isn't flying - it's boating."

The engine started with a roar and the Beaver powered across the glassy sea. Faster and faster it went, the floats thudding against the water as the wings reached for flying speed. Then crisis and recovery occurred in a matter of fractions of a second — a huge hole in the sea lay ahead, the residue of the deep wake of a shallow-bottomed tugboat that passed nearby. The pilot reached down with his right hand and yanked the flap lever as hard as he could, making the Beaver jump into the sky, claw at the morning air, then hold its altitude, such as it was.

One of the passengers said to the pilot, "This little critter sure has good pickup."

The Beaver climbed a little more and proceeded to fly over five glaciers, affording magnificent, panoramic views of the glaciers, landing on the sea in front of Taku Lodge, a fine old house, for a salmon barbecue. Cathy looked around for the resident dog, a black Labrador, famous for being a playmate of the wild bears that lived in the nearby bush.

Indeed as the Beaver took off again, this time without incident, a black bear crossed the lawn, as he always did, and proceeded to clean up the barbecue.

"That was fabulous," Cathy said to Jack, back on the ship. "These pioneer places have a special charm."

"It's another world up here, and a good one," said Jack. "For me it's mostly about the scenery — the mountains, glaciers, the sea and the whales and watching guys in little boats fishing for big salmon. I've done all the excursions and most are pretty good, with the one you did today absolutely brilliant, but I could also do another Alaska cruise without getting off the ship and still enjoy it. Of course I just like to be afloat — it's an escape."

Cathy laughed. "You can say that again. Some of our new friends have been escaping all right!"

"I tell you," said Jack, "a lot of people leave reality behind when they step on a ship. Women more so than men. They feel they can do things they won't do ashore. It's like school camp for adults."

Call it what you like, thought Cathy, but she was enjoying it.

CHAPTER 19

And then there was the last night.

There had been a jolly dinner. Ruby, no less, had bought champagne for everyone and Jack made a little speech. There was a grand parade of the waiters carrying flaming baked Alaska dessert around the dining room, and everyone sang Auld Lang Syne.

Then May and June were gone for a final fling, and Diane hurried past from her nearby table to have a nightcap at Tony's bar. Tony had also satisfied the head barman and he was expecting a permanent bar tending job with his next contract.

Nick had good news as well. He met Cathy as *Golden Odyssey* approached Vancouver under a clear, warm sky. They were on the aft deck where strictly speaking Nick should not be, but it was late and he knew the security officer on duty, a man from his hometown in Greece.

"I've just been told I'm being promoted to headwaiter. I'll be the youngest on the ship," he said excitedly.

"Oh Nick, I'm so happy for you. When do you start?"

"With my next contract — that will be next spring in the Mediterranean."

"I'll come and see you!"

"You will?"

"Nick — you know my situation. I suppose it will depend on how the world unfolds."

They held hands, then kissed — not on the lips but continental-style with their mouths barely touching cheeks. He sighed at the fragrance of her perfume; she wanted more, but held back.

"Let's keep in touch," said Cathy. "I'll write."

"Me too," said Nick. Then he squeezed her hand and left.

CHAPTER 20
Seattle

December 1982

The snow was falling gently as the postman made his way to Cathy's house. Just a few inches were lying and he walked gingerly in case there was ice underneath. Another path with no man to clear it, he thought uncharitably. Then, as if Tom had been reading his mind, Cathy's son appeared at the front door with a shovel. "Hi Willie," he said breezily. "Sorry the job's not done yet. Don't move and I'll clear the way for you back to the gate."

"Hey Tom, you're a good lad. But first things first. Give this mail to your mom."

Tom took the letters, tossed them through the open front door of the house, and went to work with the shovel. "By the time I'm finished, Willie, there will be a runway long enough and clean enough for a Navy Crusader to land on."

Cathy was getting ready for work and did not hear the exchange. But as she came down the stairs she heard the scrape of Tom's shovel on the driveway and then saw the letters lying on the hall floor.

She picked them up and saw one was from the Navy. Cathy went into the kitchen, sat on a stool and opened it. "We regret that despite our best efforts the government in Hanoi has still not provided any information on the whereabouts of your husband. Rest assured that we will continue ..."

Cathy brushed aside a tear. What could she do?

Other wives in her situation had remarried but Cathy did not intend to give up hope. As for Tom, his belief was unshakeable − his Dad was out there, and could walk through the front door any day.

So they waited, at the same time being in touch with activist groups urging the Pentagon and the government to continue efforts to find missing servicemen in Vietnam and Laos. After the Paris Peace Accords of 1973, 591 US servicemen had been returned. But what of the 1350 listed as Prisoners of War or Missing in Action, and another 1200 Killed in Action/Body not Recovered, many of them pilots?

There was speculation that the Hanoi government was continuing to hold US servicemen to use as a bargaining tool, while others believed some had been sent to the USSR to be pumped for information, then murdered.

There were many questions, and few answers, so she would wait − wait until the snow had gone and spring arrived. But then the summer would fly by, and as the leaves turned red and gold a new winter would be round the corner.

Tom opened the front door, kicking the snow off his shoes. Then he sat down on the front step, took his shoes off, and padded into the hall. "I left the shovel outside, Mom, the forecast calls for more snow and my runway will need cleaning again for sure."

What a great kid, thought Cathy. Well, I'm not alone, not with this little character.

"Thanks Tom. Time you were getting ready for school. What's on today?"

"Oh, same old, same old — but I got some extra math from my new teacher. He says I'm one of a group doing good and he wants to give us some advanced work."

"Tom," admonished his mother, "don't say *doing good*. You've been watching those illiterates on TV, particularly sportscasters. Goodness me, they speak bad English. Please say *doing well*."

"Sure Mom." Then, seeing the letter in Cathy's hand, added, "Is that a letter about Dad?"

"It is. Still no news I'm afraid. But I'm not discouraged. Time is a great healer and the two governments, in Washington and Hanoi, seem to have more contact than they used to. You know, my Dad used to tell me about the war with Japan. I mean, at one time we and the Japanese were deadly enemies. Now we are major trading partners — think about our new TV, made in Japan."

"That reminds me, Mom. We're making Christmas cards in the art class. I'm going to do one for Dad."

"Good plan, Tom. Bring it home and we'll write a message together."

Then he was off, and Cathy put on her coat and set off for work. Life went on.

Christmas came with its round of parties, Doc's card was dispatched, with love and optimism, "care of the government, Hanoi," and soon it was the hangover month of January with its bills, bad weather and a long wait for spring. Seattle can be a dreary place in winter because of its lingering clouds and rain.

On such a day, Willie the postman arrived with a little sunshine. It was a letter from Nick. Cathy had written to him after the cruise. No sooner was she home than she realized she missed Nick. He had been good company. Already she was thinking about meeting him again. What was that old movie — *Same Time Next Year?* But this was different, or was it? Cathy's letter to him was carefully crafted to show she cared. Well, a little.

Nick had news — his promotion to headwaiter would mean a transfer to a new ship, the *Ocean Odyssey*, which was soon coming into service in the Mediterranean.

Then he made her heart miss a beat.

Will I see you on board? he asked. September would be a year since they had met, and it was a perfect month in the Mediterranean.

Cathy put the letter down. September? What am I doing in September? Then she realized she was saying this out loud, and it was if she was asking whether she should go and waiting for an answer. And the answer seemed to be yes.

The following Saturday morning Cathy dropped off Tom at the school soccer field and met Shirley at a nearby coffee bar.

"How's the boy?" asked Shirley.

"He's fine, but after a morning sloshing around on a soggy soccer pitch I'll probably have to hose him down." She paused, then added, "We got another letter from the Pentagon. Still no word. I must say it's hard not to be pessimistic."

Shirley stirred her coffee. "Had any other mail?"

"Why do you ask?"

"What about the waiter you met? Sounds like he was a regular guy — at least he might be a pen pal?"

Cathy laughed. "Pen pal — that's all I need. Well, as it happens he has just written to me, and he's been promoted and is moving to a new ship that will be in the Mediterranean this summer."

"And ..."

"And what?"

"C'mon," said Shirley, "is that all? Has he not suggested you take another cruise?"

"Yes he has. And to be honest I would love to go. I've never been to the Mediterranean and meeting up with this man — his name is Nick by the way — would be a bit of fun.

"The trouble is I feel kind of guilty. Suppose Doc comes home while I'm away — with another man! And what if anyone here heard about Nick?"

Shirley pushed aside her coffee cup and said, "Now look here. It's been 10 years since you saw Doc and the chances of his turning up while you are away can be easily explained. You have a life to lead. What he does not know will not hurt him, so just don't ever mention you have met Nick. Confessions cause more harm than good.

And your secret is safe with me — this little town will know nothing."

Cathy went home with two of Shirley's words ringing in her ears — confessions and secrets. What was she getting into?

But fate seemed to be saying she should do this cruise, for as it happened Tom was going to a Boy Scout jamboree in Colorado in September, and he would be away for two weeks. Plenty of time for her to fly to Europe, take a cruise, and return. Hey, it would be educational; here she was, a woman of 35 and had never set foot in Paris or Rome. Or Athens, she thought with a smile.

Cathy checked the Yellow Pages and quickly found Ocean Cruise Lines.

"Hi, I'd like to inquire about a cruise in the Mediterranean in September."

"I can give you information," Cathy was told, "but we don't take bookings. You'll have to do that through a travel agent."

Darn, thought Cathy. If she used the local travel agent everyone would know her business.

With that, she picked up the Yellow Pages again and checked travel agents. They were scores of them around Seattle. She picked one in an affluent suburb on the other side of the city, one that specialized in cruises, and dialed its number.

The agent she spoke to said *Ocean Odyssey*, being a new ship, was heavily booked, with two weeks in September chartered to special groups. But there was space on one cruise, 10 days from Venice to Malaga in Spain. Ports of call were Dubrovnik, Sorrento, Rome (well, the port for the city), Florence (once again its port), Portofino, St Tropez and Barcelona.

The price was right, even with the single supplement. One thing Cathy did not have to worry about was money — the US Navy paid her a good allowance, she had her job, and when her parents passed away she received a useful inheritance. Cathy was going to indulge herself a little.

Cathy told the agent to put a hold on a cabin and said she'd call her back, then went to a bookcase and found an atlas. She found the page with Spain and quickly realized that Malaga was a wonderful gateway for Granada with its Alhambra, Ronda (where the likes of Ernest Hemingway liked to visit its historic bullring) and Seville with its cathedral.

But, she thought, I'm not telling anyone I'm going on a cruise. Having been on the Alaska cruise people might think I have met someone, and I don't want my life muddied up. If it means having a secret life, then so be it.

The next day she went to the newspaper administrator's office and put in her application for leave.

"Two weeks in September? Vancouver Island's lovely then," said Peggy, who ran the department and knew everything about everyone. "That's where I'm going. And you?"

"Haven't decided yet," said Cathy, "but that's when Tom is going to a Boy Scout jamboree, so I may as well buzz off then too."

"Quite right. Let me know where you decide to go."

No way, thought Cathy.

"Of course — probably Europe. I have relatives there. In Spain, various places actually. I'll get a rail pass or rent a car."

And then she made for the door before Peggy could ask any more questions.

CHAPTER 21

It was late August and Cathy and Shirley were walking home from the pub.

"Okay," said Cathy, "everything is arranged. I'm going on the cruise but nobody except you knows that. Tom is happy going to the jamboree — deliriously excited is more like it. He's not bothered about going to Europe and is probably too young to get very much out of it right now. The story is that I'm going to look up long-lost relatives, and there's a bit of truth in that because on my mother's side there was a wayward uncle who migrated from Italy to Spain and was last heard of running a restaurant in Andalucia."

Shirley laughed. "Plenty of scope there," said Shirley. "How do we keep in touch?"

"Glad you asked that. Here is a list of all the hotels I am staying at, with phone numbers, plus the number of the ship. You can call even when it's at sea. It's expensive but I'll pay you back. Now I have a big favor to ask — can you check my house every couple of days and if you see any mail from the Pentagon please open it. If it's important — call. If a tall, dark man is in the house — call!"

The next few days were a blur as she got Tom ready for the jamboree, picked up her air and cruise tickets, and then discovered she needed a new suitcase. She went shopping and found one with a combination lock so it could be used as a safe, and there was no key to lose.

She checked Nick's last letter. He was expecting her on the ship at Venice. He would prefer to be with her for the two days she was spending in the city before boarding, but that was not possible. "Take care," he advised her. "Look out for Italian men."

That was rich, thought Cathy, coming from a Greek. But she had to admit that Nick was not typical of the sort that preyed on women. Or should that be the type that women made themselves available to, or preyed on men? She chuckled at the thought — never a dull moment in cruising.

Tom, a joy as always, gave his mother a big kiss as the Boy Scout bus drew up outside their home. "Bye Mom, don't forget to write." Then he was off, his shirttail hanging out and one shoelace undone.

Cathy waved, but he was already romping on the back seat with his pals — his holiday had begun. Hers was soon to begin.

CHAPTER 22
En route to Italy

September 1983

British Airways check-in at Seattle airport was crowded when Cathy arrived, but she skirted the main group and went to the area for first class and club class passengers. It was a long overnight flight to London and she had decided to pay the extra and go business class. Why BA called it club class she could not fathom. She wasn't in a club, nor did she want to be. She just wanted a bigger seat, more legroom, and quiet.

The flight was fine, although she found the older flight attendants in business a bit bossy — she was sure it was worse in first class. The younger, less jaded flight attendants worked the economy section, but Cathy was prepared to put up with English frostiness for nine hours.

She had a gin and tonic, a glass of red wine with the meal — the vegetarian option, which she had pre-ordered, not because she didn't eat meat, but because it was usually the best food. The sun was setting over the Rocky Mountains as she prepared for the night. The window blind closed, Cathy put the seat back as far as it would go, closed her eyes, and pulled the blanket tightly around her neck.

Then she wondered what tomorrow would bring.

Pilots like London's Heathrow airport because of the quality of the air traffic controllers. Cathy lost count of the shops in the terminal and found herself thinking she had somehow landed in a shopping mall. Out of curiosity she stopped at a camera store because it had a big poster promoting the camera she had just bought in Seattle.

The price — duty free — was considerably more than she had paid for the camera in Seattle, and that was with state and federal taxes. "Can I help you madam?" asked a silvery-voiced salesman.

"Yes please," said Cathy with her sweetest Sunday smile. "Can you direct me to the British Airways business class lounge?"

"Right over there," said the salesman.

Cathy decided that shopping was not a good idea, not right here anyway, and resolved to be on her guard when she got to continental Europe. Then she walked over to the BA lounge and showed her ticket.

"Your flight to Venice is in two hours and on time. Make yourself comfortable," said the agent.

Cathy walked in to find a large room almost filled with passengers, mostly men on business judging by their briefcases and serious expressions as they buried themselves in newspapers.

"Anyone sitting here?" she said politely to such a person, who grunted something sounding affirmative. Well, she thought, I doubt if he's going to Venice.

She put her flight bag on a seat and went to get a coffee. There was cake so she took a piece, and then selected a newspaper from a rack nearby. The choice was large — from the weighty-looking *Telegraph* and *Times* to tabloid papers with similar-looking red tops.

"You American?" said a voice, which went on, "I hope I'm not being a pain but I gather by the way you are looking at the newspapers that you are not familiar with the press here. Can I recommend the *Daily Telegraph*? It has good coverage of world news and most of the people in the photographs are properly dressed."

Cathy laughed. "I know what you mean. Yes I am American, and I also work for a newspaper, so I have heard of the terrible tabloids and the nearly naked Page Three girls. I was looking for a good paper with world news but I'm also interested in the London theatre — what's new and what's on and that sort of thing."

"Ah, the *Telegraph* has good coverage of the theatre, cinema, and the arts. Also there will be at least half a page of advertisements listing what shows are running. You might also try *Time Out* magazine — see, over there."

"You're very kind," said Cathy, looking directly at this young man with curly hair and a kind, expressive face. "Where are you from?"

"Scotland — Ayr to be exact, home of Robert Burns the poet, *honest men and bonny lassies* and all that. But look, have you got a seat in this madhouse?"

"Sort of," said Cathy, thinking I'd rather sit with this guy.

"Where are you?"

"I'm on a settee with room for one more — over there."

Cathy said she would join him. She retrieved her bag and headed for the settee.

"I'm Robin," said her new friend. "Robin Atkinson. And you?"

"Cathy, from Seattle and heading for Venice."

"Me too. What are you doing there?"

"Well I've got two nights in a hotel and then I'm on a cruise ship to Malaga."

"Not the *Ocean Odyssey*?"

"Yes, the very one!"

"Me too."

Robin went on to explain that he was a golf professional hired by the cruise line to explore the possibilities of introducing a golf program for passengers. Thanks to Arnold Palmer and Jack Nicklaus golf was becoming more popular and golfers, generally well-educated with good jobs, were a market they wanted to target.

"Mind you," said Robin, "there are not a lot of golf courses until we get to Spain, where I'm going to look around after we arrive, but I also want to see if there's a place on the deck for a golf net, and talk to passengers on whether they would like to play. What about you?"

"Count me in. I've always enjoyed watching the game on TV but haven't got round to picking up a club. Mind you a girlfriend of mine has just started, although I would not say she is a true golfer. I mean, I said to her she was spending a lot of time at the local course and she replied, *well, that's where the men are.*"

"Aye, but they are so one-minded about the game, most of them, that they wouldn't notice if Brigitte Bardot stepped on to the first tee.

"Anyway, maybe there will be a chance to give you an introductory lesson or two. I've got a few clubs, men's and women's, with me."

CHAPTER 23
The Mediterranean Cruise

When they got to Venice the sea was in — literally. The old city was having one of its periodic floods and was awash.

Robin phoned Cathy from his hotel. "Nae golf here today but my hotel's dry. What about yours?"

"Fine here too. St Mark's Square is flooded but I hear there are wooden walkways."

"Oh aye, they're used to that here. Tell you what — get your wellies on and I'll come over and pick you up and we'll do some exploring."

Cathy said, "Get what on?"

"Yer wellies — Wellington boots, so named after the Duke of Wellington who wore them at the Battle of Waterloo. Actually it didn't rain that day but ... sorry I'm blethering on. See you in 30 minutes."

Cathy had brought a pair of what her mother would have called sensible walking shoes and these she retrieved from the bottom of her suitcase. Her wallet, less a little cash and one credit card, went into the suitcase along with her passport and travel tickets, and she spun the combination.

The cash and credit card she put in a slim purse, which she slipped inside her brassiere. Right, Cathy thought, I'm ready for Europe.

Robin was waiting downstairs.

"Hullo there, pal," he said. "Nice place this. Better than mine — I think Marco Polo slept in my room — the bed for sure. It's shaped like a banana."

Cathy laughed. "I've heard that in Venice not all hotels are created equal. Are you a true Scot looking for a bargain?"

"I wish I was a mean Scot, and then maybe I'd have more money. No, a pal who used to live in Venice recommended my place. Anyway, it's just for two nights, not for life."

The sun was just breaking through the cloudy sky as they turned into St Mark's Square, which indeed was under water. Duckboards had been laid down and a long line of tourists was waiting to get into the cathedral.

"Tell you what," said Robin, "it's almost lunchtime. What do you say if we come back tomorrow morning, and early, when it should be easier to get straight into the cathedral? It really is majestic inside and I could easily spend the morning there, and hopefully see most of it before the tour buses arrive. What about lunch right now?"

"Sure. I'm so happy to be here I had forgotten about lunch. Let's do like the Italians and have a pizza."

And so they found a pleasant restaurant where they had their pizza, and a glass of mellow Veneto red wine, then they strolled to the lagoon. Some walkways were under water but they were able to navigate a path, stopping occasionally to take in the sights.

Cathy checked her guidebook, looked at a church door, and said to Robin, "Let's go in here. This is a historic place. Handel was organ master."

When they left Cathy was feeling jetlagged, so she went back to her hotel with a loose arrangement to meet for dinner. "I'll take a nap and call you," she said.

It turned out to be 10 PM when she awoke. "I'm so sorry," Cathy told Robin on the phone. "I've just woken up and really don't want to go out now. I'm going to get a room service snack and try to sleep off my jetlag."

"Good idea, and no problem. Let's meet early tomorrow — I'll pick you up at 8 AM. We can have breakfast and beat the crowds to St Mark's."

CHAPTER 24
Exploring Venice

They were the first to enter the great cathedral. "See me," said Robin, "none of my pals would ever believe I'd be up at the crack of dawn to see a cathedral, but then none of those heathens have been here, nor could they understand the majesty and the history of this place."

Cathy and Robin spent the morning there, then tiptoed on the duckboards to the lagoon where the shuttle to the Cipriani Hotel was waiting.

"Reservation, sir?" asked the boatman, smartly dressed in blazer and cap. Yes, Robin had booked a table for lunch.

They stepped aboard the sleek motorboat and in 10 minutes were stepping ashore at the Cipriani's dock. Inside, the general manager Dr. Rusconi was waiting, as always, and after handshakes a waiter stepped forward with two Bellini's — prosecco and peach juice.

"This is rather spiffy," said Cathy. "You come here often?"

"Never in my life," said Robin, "but it's said to be one of the two best places in Venice. Well, that's not including all the monuments, canals, bridges, churches, shops and so on. Mustn't forget them."

They were shown to a table by the pool. "I gather it is the only hotel pool in Venice," said Robin, "and it's big, eh? But what is remarkable about this place, they say, is that they cut the grass by hand rather than use a lawn mower with a noisy engine. I call that class."

"You remind me of a travel writer I know — Jack Silver," said Cathy. "He has been everywhere and is a great man for detail."

"Oh I haven't been to that many places, but I do read a lot. I suppose I'm pretty good at preparation. When I go to a place I hate to miss out on anything."

"You're off to a good start here," said Cathy.

They had a simple lunch of fresh pasta with more of that delicious Veneto wine.

"Let me share the check please," said Cathy afterwards.

"No, my treat," said Robin, taking out his wallet.

"Listen — pal," said Cathy. "I can talk like a Scotsman too. I can also pay my way, which I would rather do. I work for a living just as you do and anyway I prefer to go 50-50 rather than take turns. It's too easy to forget who paid the last time."

"But it's not a lot — we chose sensibly and the bill is quite reasonable."

"All the more reason for me to share this one then," laughed Cathy, reaching into her sweater for her money.

"I see you're taking no chances with the Italians," said Robin, then, returning to the theme, went on, "I have to admit you are right. As we say in Scotland, you pay your way and you keep your friends."

"Okay, friend," said Cathy, "here's my share. Now, what was the other place on your restaurant list?"

"Ah," said Robin, "that's Harry's Bar. If you want to go there I'm up for that, but we'll never get a table now. But sometimes you can sit at the bar where the atmosphere is always good. Also, sharing the bill at Harry's Bar is not a problem with me. Either that or I take out a second mortgage."

The rest of the afternoon was spent strolling the narrow streets of Venice, guidebooks in hand. At first they picked out specific churches or monuments to visit, but they kept coming across other treasures, some of which were in their books and some that were not. In the end they just wandered, soaking up the atmosphere of the old streets and canals.

They had done almost a full circle and had got to the lagoon near the Bridge of Sighs when a gondola approached. There was a group on board, probably a family, and several excited children. "What do you think?" said Robin. "Shall we do the ultimate tourist thing? It's expensive."

"Why not?" replied Cathy, turning to Robin. "What would I tell my son? It's probably the only thing he knows about Venice."

The words were hardly out of her mouth when there was a commotion from the gondola and a scream. As the gondola turned into the lagoon it rocked as it ran into the wake of a passing vessel.

And a child fell into the water.

Robin did not hesitate, running to the edge of the quay and jumping in. The others in the gondola screamed frantically as Robin bobbed to the surface and looked around.

"Over there," they shouted. It was in Greek but Robin got the message. He could see they were pointing behind him, and when he spun himself around he could see a small girl, just her head and one arm above the water.

Heavens, it was cold, and the swollen water was rough and tasted surprisingly salty. Robin spat out a mouthful and swam strongly towards the girl, who disappeared under the surface when he was about 6 feet away. He took a deep breath and dived, kicking hard with his legs and reaching out with his hands.

Got her! Robin's left hand found a shoulder. He put his right hand under her other arm and pushed for the surface.

The girl was not heavy. He thought she must be about five. But she was terrified, and flailed her arms and kicked with her legs as he struggled to keep her head above water.

Then he saw the life ring. Cathy had thrown it and Robin was able to grasp it and hang on until another gondola came to them. Willing arms reached down, pulled the girl to safety — then an arm was offered to him.

By this time Robin had seen they were close to some steps, so he backed off, and with a handful of brisk strokes reached the side of the lagoon, and pulled himself up the steps.

"My hero!" said Cathy, rushing up to Robin.

"More like a big drip," said Robin, "and a cold one. I'm going to scoot back to the hotel for a hot bath."

Then they saw the second gondola tie up nearby. They went over to check on the girl and saw she was all right. The first gondola then arrived, and people poured off it, one a woman who ran up to Robin.

"Thank you so very much for saving my niece. You are a brave man."

Then, noticing the Ocean Cruise Line label on Cathy's bag, she added, "Are you passengers on the *Ocean Odyssey*?"

"Well, yes we are. We get on tomorrow."

"I know. The captain is my uncle, and the girl your friend has saved is his daughter. I must know your names."

Well, thought Robin as he squished his way to the hotel, that should be worth a bottle of Metaxa if I get pneumonia.

CHAPTER 25

Hours later, Robin and Cathy walked into Harry's Bar.

"Good evening," said Robin, "We don't have a reservation but perhaps you have a table, or we could eat at the bar?"

"Mr Atkinson — we have been expecting you," said the maître d'. "We have had a message from a very good customer, Captain Criticos of Ocean Cruise Line. He is deeply grateful to you for saving the life of his youngest daughter, and he thought as you were British you would be coming here tonight. So we have for you and your friend the best table in the house and a bottle of champagne. Come this way."

With that he held out his arm for Cathy, who smiled to Robin, and took the maître d's arm for the walk to the table as the waiters, barmen and — with ready enthusiasm — the customers, applauded the hero of the lagoon.

"Cheers," said Cathy holding up a flute of champagne, "this looks like being another interesting cruise."

The next day, Robin walked into his cabin on *Ocean Odyssey* and said to the steward with his bags, "surely there has been a mistake."

It was huge, more like a suite. On a table was a bouquet of flowers, a box of chocolates, a bowl of fruit and an ice bucket with a bottle of champagne.

"The captain arranged this?"

"Yes sir, and he asked me to call him when you boarded."

Five minutes later there was a knock on the door. It was the captain.

"Mr. Atkinson," he beamed, "you did a wonderful thing yesterday and I want to thank you with all my heart."

He held out his hand, then changed his mind, stepped forward and wrapped his arms around Robin, giving him a big bear hug.

"I shall personally see to it that you have the cruise of your life."

"Look Captain, I only did what you or any other person, man or woman, would have done in the same circumstances. But thanks anyway for arranging for the good night at Harry's Bar, and thanks for the lovely suite — and all the gifts."

"That stuff is routine — it goes, in varying degrees, to many other passengers. But I have something special with me that is just for you."

And he held out a bottle of Metaxa.

"I'll have a drink with you later. Right now I have to get this ship out of Venice. Goodbye for now, Mr. Atkinson."

And with that he was gone.

Cathy did not go to the ship with Robin as she wanted to spend the morning shopping for shoes. How she adored Italian shoes, and although the prices were astronomical they were far less than she'd pay at home. And, of course, they would always be the shoes from Venice.

Not wellies, she thought with a laugh to herself. What she did find was a pair of simple black leather shoes that were light and elegant — just right for dancing. The previous evening's conversation had touched on Robin's enthusiasm for the dance floor, and she was looking forward to some of that.

She liked this man. Another friend like Jack Silver, she thought. Nick? He was special.

Hey, hang on old girl, what's this? Reviewing your love life? Definitely not! Your social life? Nope. But, it must be said, thought Cathy as she stopped at a café, life is looking up.

She sat down and ordered a cappuccino, then stepped over to a kiosk next door and bought a newspaper; it was that day's *International Herald-Tribune*. She leafed through it quickly and found nothing. Would she ever see the story she was waiting for? Would Doc be on Page One, all smiles and on his way home? One day.

Cathy finished her coffee. Superb — but then she was a convert to the Starbucks revolution, which had started in 1971 in Seattle's Pike Place Market. She resolved to make a point of finding a good cup of coffee wherever *Ocean Odyssey* took her. Not a big deal, but she was a woman of habit — she liked her coffee in the morning. Just a cup. But why not have the best? Why not indeed?

Then she found herself navigating the narrow streets back to her hotel. She had already paid the bill and checked out, so it was simply a matter of collecting her luggage from the concierge, crossing his palm with silver, and getting to the ship.

The concierge had thought of that. He had a friend with a private boat who could give her a little tour of the canals and drop her and her luggage right at the ship. The price was right, so it was a deal.

Cathy's bags were taken to the motorboat where she met Antonio, a handsome fellow in trousers so tight it reminded her of a ski instructor who graded such garments — some hip-huggers showed the wallet, others revealed a coin in the back pocket, but the real McCoy's were those where you could read the dates on the coins. Antonio's were of the latter variety.

Off they went, round a corner and all of a sudden they were in a bigger canal with gondolas doing their business. Handsome buildings with intricate carvings and cupolas went by, although the water was so high some people had sandbags on their steps. Then into a bigger canal and here were vaparettos, the water buses of Venice.

This was the Grand Canal, a bustling place where people went about their lives as Venetians had for hundreds of years. Cathy sat dreaming about Marco Polo and imagined Silk Route merchants in flowing robes on this very waterway.

Then they were in the lagoon and the ship lay dead ahead. *Ocean Odyssey* looked superb, gleaming white and very modern. It was a new ship — straight out of the box, as Robin had said in his British way.

The boatman tied up at steps 50 yards from the ship and carried her luggage to the walkway, then whistled for a crewman to come with a trolley.

In no time Cathy was aboard and clutching a glass of champagne. "Welcome aboard," said a smiling young man. "I have a message for you."

Cathy put down the glass and ripped open the envelope.

It was from Nick. "Lovely to have you back. I'm busy all day. See you at dinner. You have a good table in my area! Nick."

It was as she expected. Sailing day was always mayhem for crew, and with Nick in a responsible new job she knew he would be going flat out.

No problem, a girl had to unpack, find her way around the ship and that sort of thing.

Her cabin was beautiful — bright with a big window, and with a settee and table. It was more like a suite, definitely a step above what she had paid for. Thank you Nick, she thought. On the table were a bouquet of flowers and a bottle of wine in an ice bucket. There was also a note from the captain (he of the flowers) and from her travel agent (she of the wine). Cathy was delighted to see that Captain Criticos was in command.

Her bags arrived just as the emergency drill was called. She was tired after that; it might have been the jetlag, or the thought of unpacking. Either way she put a Do Not Disturb sign on the door and lay down.

CHAPTER 26

Ocean Odyssey nudged out of the Venice lagoon and pointed its bow southwards into the Adriatic. As it did so, it collected a wave, nothing much really, but enough to wake Cathy in her cabin. She looked at her watch, got up and stepped into the bathroom.

My, this was an improvement on the old ship, which just had a shower. Cathy looked around at a spacious area with a proper bathtub — not full size but not bad. It also had a shower attachment that could be unhooked so she could wash her hair in the bath.

And the amenities! They were the best name-brand French, but oh-la-la, the print! Cathy was a young woman with good eyesight but even she had to struggle to read the names on the bottles. How is an old guy, she wondered, going to find the shampoo bottle when he is in the shower? Okay, he should check before he runs the water, but don't most people go into a bathroom without their glasses? She resolved to make a note of that in her comment card.

Ah, the comment card — before the end of each cruise every passenger was implored to fill in a detailed questionnaire about the ship's services and personnel. Cathy would never forget that on her last cruise she was asked for her opinion (and had to score 1 to 10) on a bewildering number of crew, some of whom she had never met, such as the cocktail pianist and the padre. How many souls had he saved? Just four? Give him four out of 10!

Jack Silver had told her about a French hotel manager whose practice was to send only the complimentary comment cards to the head office. "Ze others," he said with a flourish, "they go over the side."

Cathy unwrapped the soap, which had a delicate fragrance of frangipani. The towels were soft and fluffy, and she noted the end of the toilet tissue was folded into a triangular shape. The steward's work presumably.

Cathy playfully wondered about this: was that not an invasion of her privacy? Why should the steward know of her every movement, so to speak? She resolved to make a little triangle herself after every visit.

There was a knock on the door. Speak of the devil, thought Cathy, and sure enough, there was the steward. "My name is Dan, and I'm from Manila."

"Hi, my name is Cathy and I'm from Seattle."

"Do you have any special requests, miss?"

Cathy liked that — "miss." Someone out there doesn't see me as an old gal.

"Not really. I'm easy to look after, no breakfast in bed and that sort of thing. One thing — is there a Laundromat on this ship?"

"Certainly is, miss, just down the corridor to your left and on your right. I should tell you it gets very busy in there. On the last cruise we had a problem with one passenger who arrived with a big bag of dirty laundry and a sign saying Out of Order. She then reserved one of the machines by putting the sign on it."

"No? What a nerve!" said Cathy.

"But she got found out by the housekeeper who was very upset. Housekeeper is a very tough woman."

"I'll be sure to avoid her," said Cathy sternly. "As for you, don't put any candies on my pillow at night — too much caffeine late in the day and I'll be out of order."

Cathy consulted the brochure on her desk, which gave the deck plan of the ship. She was looking for the Athena dining room. There it was — on deck 5 just behind the reception area and the Acropolis bar. She was on deck 7, port side, slightly aft of center, so that meant she had to go out of her cabin, turn right, first left and down two sets of stairs — old salts would say companionways.

Cathy enjoyed at least knowing if not using the correct nautical terms as it was part of the fun of being at sea. She even enjoyed a little rough weather when the ship rolled and pitched because it reminded her that she was on a vessel and not staying at a hotel.

But no whales on the carpet here, she noted as she stepped into the corridor. When she got to the top of the stairs her attention was drawn to a large picture, particularly to the price tag at the bottom. Oh no, she thought, not another art auction!

Then she saw one more price tag, and yet another. Every picture was for sale. She was captive in a floating art saleroom.

The bar was quiet. It was the first night and only a few of the passengers were in the room, none of whom seemed to be aware of a woman pianist dolefully playing in the corner. Sounds like she's got jetlag too, thought Cathy.

"Drink, madam?"

She knew that voice. It was Tony.

"How nice to see you," said Cathy.

"And pleased to have you on board." Then, lowering his voice, he added, "Nick's waiting for you in the dining room."

"Of course. See you later."

As she got to the end of the bar she recognized Diane, the married woman from Florida. "Hi," said Diane breezily.

"Well hello," said Cathy. "Fancy meeting you on this ship."

"I could say the same."

So much for her secret cruise, though Cathy, who walked on into the dining room and looked for Nick.

CHAPTER 27

"Hello Mrs. Robertson," said Mike Brown, the maître d'. "We meet again on the beautiful new *Ocean Odyssey*."

"Lovely to see you, Mike," said Cathy. "What a fabulous dining room. You must be very proud to be here. *Ocean Odyssey* is much bigger."

"It is a bigger ship and a bigger job. And yes, I am proud of this room, and also my team. Let me introduce you to my newest headwaiter."

Nick arrived right on cue. "Good evening," he said warmly with a slight bow.

Cathy's eyes sparkled as she looked at the tall, young man in the splendid dinner jacket. His wavy, dark hair had been cut by an expert and made him look very polished and professional. There was a light tan acquired from the winter's cruising, and he looked well-prepared for the job ahead — or any movie set requiring a leading man.

"Can I take your arm?"

Cathy was enchanted. She stepped forward, put her arm through his and he walked her to her table. She squeezed his arm and whispered, "I'm so happy to see you."

"Me too. It's been a long time."

"See you after dinner?"

"Yes, I'll finish about 10:30. Go to the promenade deck, aft, and I'll meet you there."

Cathy's table was by the side. They came around a pillar and saw Robin was there, and Jack Silver.

"Jack! What a pleasant surprise. But of course it's a new ship; and you're back at work."

"It's a tough job but someone has to do it," said Jack, extending his hand. He pulled Cathy forward and kissed her on both cheeks. "We're in Europe so I get extra kisses."

Cathy greeted Robin and sat down. "Who's our number four?" she asked.

Her question was answered with the arrival of Diane. "Hi guys," she said, flashing her eyes at Jack and Robin. Cathy might as well have been invisible.

"Well this is a cozy little group," said Jack, standing up. "Just four of us. Older ships had a lot of big tables but *Ocean Odyssey* has a good number of smaller ones too, which I prefer myself."

"I just hope they don't forget about us behind that pillar," said Robin.

"No danger," said Jack with a knowing smile. "We have two well-connected women with us."

"You got that right," said Diane. "Here, our wine's on the way. I'm assured it's the best."

No doubt, thought Cathy. No doubt.

The dinner was a great success with Jack and Robin hitting it off right away. Jack was delighted when he heard Robin was from Scotland.

"Old Scotia is one of my favorite countries," said Jack enthusiastically. "It has everything — castles, whisky, golf, Edinburgh, Skye, and there's nobody there. Just fly in, rent a car, and in 20 minutes you can be out in the country or by Loch Lomond."

"You're very kind," said Robin, "but I have to concede that the weather is not always cooperative."

"Nonsense," said Jack with a flourish. "If it rains you visit one of the wonderful galleries or museums in Edinburgh or Glasgow, and I'll tell you something else — that a little light rain, what you call drizzle, adds a moodiness to Glencoe or Skye. Have you been to Dornoch?"

"Of course," said Robin. "The golf course there is a cracker. Donald Ross, the man who designed many fine golf courses in America, including Pinehurst No. 2, is from Dornoch. And talking of America, Dornoch is just up the road from Skibo Castle, which was built by Andrew Carnegie, the Scots boy who went to America and made a huge fortune."

"Who made a fortune?" said Diane, tuning into a word she understood.

"Andrew Carnegie," said Robin. Warming to the task, he went on, "One thing I like about Carnegie was that when Skibo was built he did not presume to join Dornoch Golf Club, as it was then; it is now Royal Dornoch. You see he did not know the game, and it may have been he could not have joined without a decent handicap.

"No, he built his own golf course at the castle where he could learn the game and practice, and took lessons. Only then did he join the club. If only it were the same today."

"I know what you mean," said Diane. "At our country club in Florida we have people who are real bad players. They take forever to go round, even with a cart."

Robin laughed. "I heard about four Americans who went to a golf course in Scotland and asked for carts. They were shocked to discover that there were no carts, and even if they brought their own, they would need medical certificates stating they needed the carts to get around.

"They were very happy to discover a golf course on the West Coast where they could have carts — no questions asked!"

"Robin, you're from Ayr? That's in the west?"

"It is indeed, home of Robert Burns — the great poet who wrote Auld Lang Syne..."

At this point Nick arrived and asked how everyone's meal was.

"Terrible," said Jack. "My serving of caviar was just half a pound, the vichyssoise was cold, and the waiter brought me lobster instead of the hamburger I ordered."

"Very sorry, sir. I will replace the meal, fire the waiter and move you to the captain's table where you will receive the best attention."

"Excellent," said Jack, getting to his feet. "Congratulations on your promotion. You look darn good in that tuxedo."

"Thank you, Mr. Silver."

"You make me look like a slob. I don't know if I like restaurants where the staff are better dressed than the customers."

"That's a good point, Mr. Silver. "Some cruise ships are moving to a more casual dress, for staff as well as passengers. Personally I don't think you need to wear a tie to enjoy a meal."

"I think you've got your head screwed on the right way," said Jack, sitting down.

Diane spoke up, "Are you the guy who makes the desserts?"

"No, that's the pastry chef, but I can make you something special like Cherries Jubilee."

"Right on," said Diane, looking round the table. "Cherries Jubilee for four?"

After dinner Cathy went up to the Promenade deck and went out on deck. It was a fine night on the Adriatic and *Ocean Odyssey* was being helped along by a light stern wind. She passed a couple lighting cigarettes and then heard a woman's giggles coming from a dark corner.

The Love Boat, she thought, does not have a monopoly.

Nick was waiting at the stern. They kissed, but quickly, and when they hugged it was like two old friends meeting. That was fine for Cathy. She was happy to see him and the feeling was mutual.

"Cathy — so glad you are here. We will have another wonderful cruise." Nick squeezed her hand.

"Yes, Nick. I had a bit of adventure getting here. I'll tell you later."

"Good idea. I have to supervise my section of the room being made up again, but I will have time off to-morrow, before lunch. I know a café in Dubrovnik. Go to the end of the main street and it's on your left. You can't miss it. Ten o'clock okay?"

"See you there." Cathy kissed him on the cheek and he was gone.

CHAPTER 28

Dubrovnik dawned fair, the medieval walled city quite a sight even to those who had been there before. Passengers stood on the deck of *Ocean Odyssey* and marveled at the huge stone blocks rising out of the sea. One of them wondered how it had been constructed. Another said the same way as the pyramids – with slaves. Somebody else joined the conversation and volunteered, "On our last cruise we took the shore excursion to the pyramids. They don't build ruins like that any more."

Cathy and Jack were passing and heard the exchange. Jack nudged Cathy playfully: "They say travel expands the mind. Sometimes I wonder."

Soon afterwards Cathy was walking into Dubrovnik. Others bought tickets and climbed steps to go along the teetering walls. What she could see at ground level was quite engrossing – a handsome city and beautifully kept. She went into a shop selling lace, then another where she bought postcards. Darn, she had forgotten to change money. But it was no problem – dollars were welcome

119

here, as they are almost everywhere cruise ships go because that is the currency of cruise ships, regardless of the nationality of the vessel.

Moments later she spotted the café Nick had spoken about, and took a table on the corner where she could see back down towards the main gate. A waiter came over, smiled at her, and presented a menu. She ordered a coffee and started to write her postcards.

Nick arrived at the same time as the coffee. "Make that two," he said to the waiter, and sat down.

"There you go again, bossing around the help."

"Give me five minutes and I'll get a Michelin star for this place."

"Oh go on. I can see the new job has gone right to your head."

They both laughed, then Cathy said, "Seriously, how is it going?"

Nick was having the time of his life. He had a tremendous job for a young man and a good boss in Mike Brown. But it was hard work because the maître d' expected maximum effort all the time. Nick had no problems with that; he always remembered his father saying that if making money was easy everyone would be rich. However, he had to be continually alert because passengers were unpredictable and some of the staff might resent his rapid promotion, particularly waiters older than him.

"Tomorrow we sail past Corfu. As you know it's my home and I would love to show it to you, but not this time. Too bad."

"Yes it is a shame, Nick. Oh well, you can always wave."

They drank their coffees, Nick paid the check and they walked slowly back towards the city gates. Cathy told him about Venice and Robin's courage in saving the captain's daughter from the lagoon. Nick had heard about it. All the crew knew and were alerted to give Robin the best of everything on board.

"How do you like your table?"

"Wonderful. Jack and Robin are great company. Diane is not really my type but she is never dull."

"You've got that right. Tony and I are sharing a cabin again but I've hardly seen him since she came on."

Said Cathy, "I can imagine him skulking around the inside of the ship then dashing across corridors in the passenger area."

"Yes, and then dragging his feet on the way back."

Cathy was on deck the next day as *Ocean Odyssey* steamed down the Adriatic. Robin came by and pointed out a speck in the distance. "That's Corfu. Nice island. No golf there, but they play cricket."

"Cricket?" said Cathy. "That's an English game, isn't it? How did it get here?"

"Who knows — Royal Navy probably. That's how cricket went to India and today it's a national passion there. Talking of India, do you like Indian food?"

"Little bit. I prefer Thai; I think the flavors are more delicate. But I don't mind an Indian curry so long as it's not too hot. I once had a Vindaloo that took off the top of my mouth."

"Better take care then if you go to Glasgow. They like their curries so hot there the city is known as Vindaloo Valley."

"Well Robin, you're probably going to have to wait till you get home for your next curry. That is, unless you ask the chef on board."

"Aye right — a Greek curry! But seriously, the chef could be from anywhere. I'll have to check. As for getting a curry ashore, you never know your luck. I was in Sweden not so long ago and had an Indian meal in Stockholm. It wasn't great, but if you're a curry addict it's a case of any port in a storm. Spain will be no problem but I'm hoping to 'currify' before then."

Several decks below two American women were looking at a chart of Europe that had been put up by the navigation officer. It showed the ship's intended itinerary and the progress to date.

"Look Betty, here's a map."

"I can't figure it out."

"Of course. I forgot — this is your first trip to Europe. Look here — the yellow bits are the land and the blue bits are the sea."

"Okay."

"See, we're here, with Italy there. We go up the coast of Italy, stop in France and go on to Spain."

"France? Nobody told me we were going to France!" exclaimed Betty. "Show me again — where is it? Do we stop in Paris?"

"Didn't your travel agent explain? We spend a day at St Tropez. It's on the French Riviera."

"Come to think of it the agent did say something about that city but I thought it was in Spain. France eh? I never thought it was around here. We'd better not drink the water."

CHAPTER 29

Ocean Odyssey parted the warm, azure seas with its bulbous bow and made effortless progress, its big diesel engines thudding away below the waterline. The chief engineer, always known as "Chief," whose station was the deck above in the control room, made a final check of the instruments before he handed over to his deputy.

Being a new ship that meant little more than a scan of the computers. The days of the oily rag were long gone, which gave him more time to think about other interests, such as romance.

He went up another deck and walked into the office of the housekeeper.

"Hi, Anna."

The housekeeper looked up, startled, and pulled a folder over the money on her desk.

"Hey, you won the lottery?"

Anna went quite red, then recovered, "You might knock, Chief. We had a collection for one of the stewardesses who is getting married and I'm doing a tally. I'll be finished in a moment. But after that I have to wash my hair before the captain's party tonight. In other words I can't talk now. See you at the reception?"

"You bet."

The Chief went up to his quarters thinking about the evening's prospects. Anna was not the most attractive woman on the ship but she had an amazing figure. Nor was she the most agreeable woman he had ever met, but when she was drunk she made love with a wild passion. Tonight she would be drinking champagne at the captain's party and she would be drunk. The trick was to get Anna back to her cabin before she drank too much and became abusive.

The captain's welcome aboard party was in full swing when Jack Silver arrived.

"Champagne, sir?"

"What champagne are you serving tonight?"

"Er, Henkell Trocken."

"You are aware that this is a German sparkling wine?"

"Yessir."

"Then go to the barman and tell him I want real champagne, from France, or I will have him arrested at the next port under trade description legislation — if the Italians have such a thing."

"Good evening, Jack. Don't tell me you can't get a beer in this brewery." It was Robin, who arrived at the same time as Cathy.

"Oh it's one of my pet peeves — cruise lines offering you a glass of champagne which turns out to be a sparkling wine, although I have to say Italy produces several very drinkable spumantes such as prosecco, which can be as good as champagne."

The waiter came back. "Pol Roger, sir, with the barman's best wishes."

"A good drop indeed. This was Winston Churchill's favorite champagne. He had a glass or three every day. Now — what are you having Cathy, and you Robin?"

"Pol Roger, of course!" they chorused.

The party was off to a good start.

Captain Criticos introduced his senior officers and wished the passengers "smooth seas," then there was the obligatory joke. He told a favorite, about the captain whose routine when he came on duty was to unlock a drawer on the bridge, study a piece of paper, then lock the drawer. He did this for 30 years without anyone else seeing that piece of paper.

Naturally many men who served under him were curious, and there came the day before he was due to retire that a daredevil young officer happened to see the captain's keys on the chartroom table. The captain had gone into the wireless room. Quickly the young officer unlocked the drawer and found the piece of paper. On it were the words — "the right hand side is starboard, and the left side is port."

Captains' dinners are not all they are cracked up to be. For a start, the captain has little say as to who is invited. Most of the guests will be regular passengers who expect to be there, and invariably are. It is simply a recognition of their loyalty — and their wealth. Some are frightful bores who have been everywhere. Well, they have visited the ports and done the shore excursions. Their world is as wide as a tour bus's turning circle.

A merry band of remarkable widows live on cruise ships. They stay on for months at a time, and when the vessel has to go into dry dock for maintenance the cruise line will send them to a five-star hotel in a limousine, pay the bill for the duration, then return them to the ship when it is ready for sea again.

Rosamund was such a person, and naturally she was to the captain's right. She was 90, had buried three husbands, and attributed her long life to good Scotch whisky. Then there was Jack Silver. A travel writer is an important person on a new cruise ship because many passengers book a vessel after reading about it in a newspaper or magazine. There was Robin, because he was a hero. And there was Cathy, because the captain insisted on having at least one attractive young woman at his table. The other five were frequent travelers who were there for their wallets rather than their charm or conversation.

The wine steward arrived at the table. It was Marco, the very man who had cruised with Cathy and Jack in Alaska. He recognized Cathy, gave her a wide smile and a wink, then got very serious. "Tonight, Captain," he intoned, "we have a very nice pinot grigio from Italy to start and a Medoc from France to follow."

Jack nudged Cathy. "Don't hold your breath for the pick of the cellar. Captains are not known for their knowledge of fine wines. They do know how to get gullible women drunk, but that's another story."

"You're bad," said Cathy, tasting the pinot grigio. "And this wine is good."

"Pinot grigio rarely fails," said Jack. "Just wait for the Bordeaux."

The table's attention was asked for by a clink of glasses and the captain wished everyone Bon Voyage.

The meal was good — caviar, lobster bisque, a sherbet, Beef Wellington, Peach Melba and cheese.

Rosamund didn't touch the wine. She had two large whiskies and appeared to be enjoying herself. Three of the others had iced tea and one — oh, how Jack cringed — drank Coke. But they may have been the lucky ones, for the red wine was a disaster. It was not corked — simply a dull wine from the hand of a poor winemaker.

Jack would have told Marco to get something else but it was not his call. As for the captain, he stuck to the white wine. Jack surmised he knew the red was not worth drinking, and in all likelihood there was nothing better on board. This, he rued, on a cruise ship visiting legendary ports in the wine-producing countries of Italy, France and Spain.

After dinner the captain, Jack, Robin and Cathy went to the nightclub. "Jack," said the captain, "I could see you were not enjoying the wine. This is something I have no control over. I have complained time and time again but they keep putting this rubbish on board. The sad fact is that most of passengers can't tell a fine Bordeaux from a corked Burgundy."

Jack knew he was right. "You're very honest. Now I'll be honest — I'd like a good cognac to make up for that Bordeaux."

"Waiter!" said the captain. "Get drinks for my friends. Anything they want. For me, I'll stick to Metaxa."

Meanwhile the disc jockey was getting ready to start the music. His name was Harry O'Hare and he was an old rocker from Cork in Ireland, a kid in the fifties when Bill Haley and the Comets breezed into Europe and left a trail of broken seats in concert halls and cinemas. Harry was playing in a skiffle group which was hastily adapted into a rock 'n' roll band that did quite well for a while. They had one big hit before the lead guitarist went on the bottle, and when the drummer fell under a bus Harry tried going solo as a singer.

He worked clubs in the north of England for a few years before his agent got him a job at sea. Harry loved being on cruise ships, and gin and tonics at crew-bar prices were central to the allure. Then there were the duty-free cigarettes. And the women who remembered his fleeting fame. When his singing voice spluttered and died the cruise line kept him on as an assistant cruise director and as disc jockey.

"Right then, me hearties," said Harry, "let's be having you on the floor!"

Robin touched Cathy on the arm, and nodded his head towards the floor. Cathy took this for an invitation to dance, and was not disappointed. In moments she could see Robin had a natural rhythm. He turned her a couple of times, then let her go back so both their arms were almost fully stretched, then coiled her back in as they pivoted on the balls of their feet. It was a classic jive sequence.

Robin was an expert and Cathy was no slouch. She was a little out of practice but it all came back to her — she and Doc had danced this way to Benny Goodman records. Now she and Robin were flying around the floor, his arm around her waist, a half turn, then a gentle push and she would spin out then he'd coil her in. As they warmed up he sent her in a loop and he went the other way, coming together with a whoop of excitement.

"Where have you been all my life?" said Robin, pulling Cathy close.

"Living under a mushroom."

"That's the wrong answer. Ye see, where I come from there's a patter as we call it — a dance hall language, in which certain statements have a set answer. It's all just a bit of fun. So when I ask you *where have you been all my life,* you say *avoiding creeps like you.*"

"That doesn't sound very funny to me."

"Well it would if you knew the characters I grew up with in Scotland. Their sense of humor takes no prisoners."

They were still dancing and Robin was leading Cathy in a double-time quickstep to a compulsive beat. They were close but Robin was not being suggestive; he was moving like a tango dancer.

But Cathy was certainly enjoying being held by a man who could make his body, and hers, move so well. The sound drove them on, eyes and hands sending signals to legs and bodies that strained one way and the other — out, back, coil, bodies touching lightly, then hard, thighs stroking ...

"Whew," panted Cathy. "My mother warned me about men like you."

"Ah, if only it were true. I do like to dance but it has not enhanced my love life. When we learned to dance at school in Scotland the boys were always told not to forget the wallflowers, the girls who were not so pretty and who would never have had a dance were it not for the unsurpassed courtesy of altruistic chaps like me.

"You'd have been all right. You would have been the belle of the ball every time. But it's true, there always was one girl or the other that I would fancy, but I spent so much time duty-dancing with the plain Janes that when it came to the end of the parties, I'd find that all the good-lookers had been taken."

"Poor chap. Well at least you did become a very good dancer. I'm afraid to ask any other questions."

The song finished and Harry announced, "Not bad for a warm-up, and I might say at this point that we'll be having a rock 'n' roll contest later."

"Aye, but no wi' me," said Robin. "C'mon, let's sit down and let Harry-boy do the talking."

Jack and the captain stood up gallantly as they returned to the table. Robin almost turned around and went back, for the next song was an old favorite — *Needles and Pins* by the Searchers.

"Harry knows his music," said Robin.

"That he does," said Jack. "I remember seeing him years ago when there used to be a lot of passenger talent nights. Harry used to get some atmosphere going by dressing up as Long John Silver — him of Treasure Island — carrying a cutlass and going around the ship bellowing, *Them's that die'll be the lucky ones!*"

Over in a corner of the nightclub the chief engineer was sitting with the housekeeper. She had drunk four large screwdrivers but was still reasonably sober. This was entirely due to the chief having instructed the barman to use half-measures of vodka in the first two drinks and none in the others.

"Chief, you really are a miserable bastard. You fuck me all you want, you say you are going to leave your wife, but you never do. I'm going to find another dick."

"There's nothing I want more than to be with you," said the Chief, "but now is not a good time. My kids are still in school and I don't want to upset them."

"Yeah, right. This will drag on and then you'll be saying you have to think of the grandchildren."

"Well, all right, Anna, find another man. But think of the fun we're had over the years, and with no complications. Marriage has ruined many a good friendship."

"Yes chief, you have a point." Then, running her hand around the inside of his thigh, she looked at him lasciviously and added, "let's go to my cabin and get to the real point."

As they left, the housekeeper by now a little unsteady on her feet, Tony was also on the move, fielding a diagram of the ship's layout as he made his way through the crew quarters. He took a crew elevator up six decks, walked aft for 20 feet, then found service door 12B. Tony checked around him for the all clear, opened the door gingerly, and looked across. Yes! Cabin 936. He put his head into the corridor then quickly reached for the doorbell, ducking back again. Diane, wearing a silk robe, was at the door in seconds. She looked both ways and whispered for him to come over, which he did like a rat going into a sewer.

Diane tore his clothes off feverishly, then removed her robe. Underneath she was wearing just La Perla underwear with a garter belt — very chic and sexy. Tony closed his eyes and muttered, "Mamma Mia!"

CHAPTER 30

The next day was perfect — sea calm, a light wind, and Cathy was on deck. "I thought I might find you here," said Nick. "Can I get you a coffee?"

"You certainly can, and tell me, what's that island over there — it looks like a volcano, and yes, there is smoke coming from the top."

"Yes Cathy, it is a volcano. The island is Stromboli. Did you ever see the movie of the same name with Ingrid Bergman? The producer was Alberto Rossellini and they had an affair which caused a great scandal."

Nick went to get her coffee and Cathy stared at the island, growing larger as the ship got closer. What a great romance that had been, although foolish as it was doomed from the start.

There but for the grace of God goes me, thought Cathy. Yet if I bump into anyone who knows me they will look at my situation on this ship, where I am constantly in the company of three men, and they are bound to think the worst.

"Your coffee Cathy — I mean madam," said Nick.

"I prefer Cathy," she said putting her hand on his. "Look, have you got time off in Sorrento?"

In fact Nick had made careful plans to have the evening free there and told her to skip dinner.

Meanwhile the big event this very day was the *grand galley buffet* - where lunch is laid out in the galley, or ship's kitchen, and passengers troop through and help themselves. But as Nick left she caught sight of two overweight women waddling across the deck. No way, she thought. There's no way I want to end up like that.

She had a brainwave — she would give lunch a miss and hit the Laundromat instead, which should not be busy then. Down she went, and sure enough there was nobody there, and one machine was free. She quickly went to her cabin to get her laundry and returned to put it in the machine. Once again she headed back to her cabin, but this time, as she turned a corner, she almost bumped into Dan, her steward. He looked distressed.

"Dan, what's the matter? You're crying."

"I can't tell you miss, I mean madam."

"Yes, you can. Here, come into my cabin and we'll have a little talk."

Filipino men are small so it was not difficult for Cathy to lead Dan into the cabin and sit him down. Cathy opened her fridge, took out some water and poured two glasses.

"Now — what's the problem?"

"It's the housekeeper, Anna. She won't renew my contract. All the money I make goes home to my family — I have five children in school, my mother is sick and there are big hospital bills."

"But you are doing a wonderful job," said Cathy, putting her arm around him. "I can't imagine why she would not keep you on."

"There's nothing you can do," said Dan, who was now weeping into the paper towels he had put in Cathy's cabin just that morning. "She's the boss. She does want she wants."

Cathy put her arm around Dan. "We'll see about that."

CHAPTER 31

Ocean Odyssey anchored off Sorrento beside another cruise ship, a state of affairs that did nothing for the early morning disposition of Captain Criticos. "You," he barked at the first officer, "keep any eye on that other ship and if it moves an inch closer to us let me know immediately. A collision at sea is bad enough but to be hit by another vessel while at anchor could ruin my day."

His other concern was congestion at the port with tenders from both vessels competing for limited landing space. Last time he was here, on a cruise to Athens, two old women mistakenly got on the tender for another cruise ship and nearly ended up in Alexandria.

Cathy went ashore with Jack and wandered the narrow streets of the old town. It was thronged with people buying the kind of souvenirs that end up in attics and basements. The alternative was to sit at a sidewalk café and watch the world go by, although she soon realized that the passing parade was 95 percent cruise ship passengers gawking at her.

"Ah, the joys of modern tourism," said Jack with a resigned smile as they sipped coffees. "Really, the place to
be in the summer, in the Med, is out on the water. There
you have a cool breeze, room to move and quiet. But man
is a social animal, and we are all drawn to shore even just
to see how awful it is. Just wait till we get to Florence.
Mind you, there are some important things to do ashore
— like shopping."

"Yeah right, Jack," said Cathy. "You never struck me
as a shopper."

"It's true. Check the price of that bottle of whisky over
there. It's half the price you'll pay in America and also
cheaper than the booze on board the ship. In the bad old
days before ships got computers, the barmen used to buy
booze here and sell it on board instead of the ship's inven-
tory. Many of them got rich from the proceeds. I'll tell you
about one guy I met.

"I was at this restaurant in Tuscany. I went with a
friend who knew the owner, an Italian who had been at
sea. It was a very nice place; in fact it must have cost a fair
chunk of money. So when the owner came by and I was
introduced I said to him he had clearly had a good career
afloat to be able to afford this place. I said he must have
been a captain.

"Hell no," said the restaurant owner. "I was a barman."

Jack took another drink of his cappuccino and went
on, "see that plastic card you have? It's your identity card
but it's also a charge card. With that you can buy anything on the ship, from a gin and tonic to a bingo card to a
sweater in the gift shop. You can pay for your photog-

raphy with it, have a massage and even get money at the casino — which you'll inevitably give back. You don't need cash on board; in fact you can't use cash, which means the crew can't steal. Bar fiddles and bingo rip-offs are a thing of the past."

"Bingo rip-offs?" queried Cathy.

"Sure — it used to be you paid cash for your bingo card and the cruise director paid out maybe 60 or 70 percent of the takings. The rest he shared with the purser and one or two pals. Some of these guys did very well, the smart ones salting money away in foreign bank accounts and the dumb ones building big homes that were a dead giveaway.

"When you think about it, bingo used to be seen as a simple game providing mild entertainment for the passengers. It was a service in a way, but when cruise directors began to sport Rolexes the bean-counters got to hear about it, and then after computers came in bingo became a profit center for the cruise line."

"You're such a cynic, Jack," said Cathy. "The cruise lines have got to make their money somewhere."

"That's right. You hear complaints about the cost of the transfer from Livorno to Florence, and if you have an independent spirit there are trains. But you can't find a taxi to take you to the station, or back again. So — take the excursion!"

"Thanks for telling me. Right now I'm going back to the ship. You too?"

"You carry on. I want to find a shop with newspapers."

Cathy strolled down to the dock where she found two tenders, one from *Ocean Odyssey* and one from the *Pacific Princess*. The security officer from the *Pacific Princess* was talking to an American who wanted on his tender.

"But sir, you are a passenger on the other ship."

"I know that. Can we visit your ship — just for lunch? I'll pay."

"Sorry sir, that's not allowed. I don't make the rules. Fact is we can't take your money."

"Well I tell you," said the American, "these Greeks don't know how to make a hamburger. We just thought we'd see if the Brits can do any better."

"If the truth he known, sir, our cooks are Filipino and Indian. If we could get you on board you might get a very nice curry."

"Yuk — can't stand that stuff."

"Tell you what sir, have you tried the food right here? This is Italy after all, and right behind you there's a restaurant where you'll get a plate of real spaghetti or a pizza."

"No way, never touch foreign food. I tell you, the more I see the world the more I like the good old USA."

He wandered off reluctantly and Cathy presented her ID card to the *Ocean Odyssey* security officer. "Takes all kinds, eh?"

"I wonder," said the security officer with a resigned look, "why they let him out."

CHAPTER 32

As evening fell Cathy returned to a different Sorrento. Most of the cruise ship passengers had disappeared, back on board having the meals they had paid for. Instead the town was filled with Italians, families mostly, taking the cool, night air that came with a fragrance of flowers, pasta and laughter.

Nick was waiting for her, as arranged, at the café opposite the fountain. He bounded to his feet when he saw her, a happy man. "Welcome to Italy, land of smiles."

"Lovely to be here, and with you," Cathy found herself saying.

Nick suggested having a glass of wine at the café, and then going to a restaurant he knew. They both had pinot grigio, Italy's light and fruity white wine, then strolled along a street that was for pedestrians only. Shops were open and there were a lot of people about.

"Look," said Nick suddenly, "there's Anna, the housekeeper. Just ahead of us."

Just then Anna turned into a shop. It was Cartier, the jeweler.

Cathy took Nick's arm and held him back. "Wait a moment," she whispered.

Cathy went over to the window. Anna was looking at watches. She seemed to know what she was after. In fact she quickly picked out a watch and then produced a roll of cash. Cathy gasped when she saw the money — it looked like thousands of dollars.

"Sorry about that," said Cathy to Nick. "I don't normally spy on people. But I don't think she's my favorite person right now." And she told Nick the story about Dan her steward.

Then they were at the restaurant. From the enthusiastic welcome they received, Cathy could guess Nick had been there before. "It's actually the crew choice," said Nick as he looked at the menu. "We try to keep some restaurants to ourselves so we can hide from the passengers."

"Can't say I blame you," said Cathy. She looked around the room and saw just two other couples, then a table of four in a corner. None were from the ship. The waiters moved silently among the candlelit tables, the conversation of the diners muffled by heavy scarlet curtains. It was a place for lovers of good food and wine. Maybe more.

When the wine arrived Nick squeezed Cathy's hand. "Good to be here with you."

Cathy raised her glass, looked into his eyes and spoke from her heart. "Nick, I was just thinking the same thing.

You are a lovely man and I appreciate the time you are spending with me."

"Hey, don't make it sound like this is a duty," admonished Nick. "This situation suits us both. You have a husband but he is not here. I am on my own because I choose to be at this stage of my life while I am working hard, making money and traveling. It's perfect. Mind you," and he took her hand again, "I have to warn you that I am a romantic. Please tell me — tell me at any time — if I am embarrassing you. I'm sure people can tell by my, what do you call it, my body language that I enjoy being with you."

Cathy did not care. She was a long way from Seattle, her neighbors and the busybodies at the newspaper. Her situation at home was that of a widow who had to act out her life as a watchful community thought she should. Now, for a couple of weeks, she had a life of her own, perhaps not the normal family life she might be having with Doc, but it was a real life where she could do what she wanted.

"Nick, your language is perfect, body and soul."

The meal was Italian magic, and so was the moonlight as they walked back to the ship.

Robin walked into the cramped office of the cruise director. "Mind your head on that giraffe," said John Dean. "He's my friend from Hong Kong. His name is George."

"Is that right — a Chinese giraffe? Next thing you'll be telling me the captain's got an Irish kangaroo."

John laughed. "The more you travel the more you see daft things. I mean, you'll find giraffe carvings not just in

Africa but all over the planet. Anyway I can't have a dog on the ship so I have George."

"Very well, can I talk to you about my golf nets? As you probably know I'm on board to do a report on the feasibility of offering golf as a shore excursion. We might also want to have a golf pro on board and a golf net as well. I've been up on the top deck, and right beside the funnel on the port side there's a place to put a golf net. It's a fairly simple structure."

"Sounds good to me. You'd better check with the Chief to make sure it's all right from a technical point of view. Maybe the bridge boys as well, to get their blessing."

"Will do, John."

Robin bumped into Jack Silver coming out of the office. "What ho," said Robin, "time for a beer?"

"Is the sun over the yardarm?" asked Jack. "Yes it is, in Tokyo. I'm buying — I want to hear about this golf project."

They made their way to the midships bar where Tony was mixing a Bloody Mary for Diane.

"Hi guys," she said cheerfully. "Anyone interested in an eye-opener?"

"Why not, but we can't join you. Sorry — men's talk," said Jack.

Jack nudged Robin to follow him and they headed for a table in the corner.

"Who's the wee stotter?"

"The what?"

"I should explain this uniquely Scottish term. A wee stotter usually describes a person with some merit, in this case a woman you wouldn't rush to get away from."

"Well you have to forget that one. She's a rich married woman who is here expressly for some horizontal recreation with Tony the bartender."

"Nice work if you can get it."

"Absolutely. I'm sure her husband is ostensibly on a golfing trip, but is in fact spending quality time with his mistress or girlfriend. Everyone is happy — for the time being. Then the mistress will start to feel insecure and want more of his time, and after that divorce. Next thing they're talking divorce, and that's no fun."

"Sounds like you've been there."

"Indeed I have, and I don't recommend it. Changing wives is one thing, but the children invariably suffer — but don't get me started, Robin. Let's talk golf."

Robin outlined the cruise line's plan. Research in America had shown that it was the wives who made the vacation plans, but when a cruise was suggested there was often resistance from the husbands.

"I can imagine," said Jack. "As women get older they become more adventurous. Men just get older."

The cruise line's thinking was that if a woman could tell her husband that he could play golf while on the ship he might be more inclined to give it a try. Robin explained that golf courses could be found on almost every itinerary. "Mind you, it gets hard up the Amazon and in Antarctica."

"Interesting, very interesting. What's the best cruise for golf?"

"I have to say Scotland. You can anchor off my hometown of Ayr and play Turnberry, Royal Troon, Prestwick, Glasgow Gailes and more. It's a golfer's paradise. Hawaii is very good as well, and if you'e on an Alaska cruise you can stop off at Vancouver and play at Whistler, a great spot in the mountains. Same with this cruise: near Malaga you have Spain's famous Costa del Golf with Valderrama and Aloha Golf Club, among 50 courses to play and enjoy."

"Cruising and golf — that could make a good article."

"Be my guest and write it. I'll give you all the help I can. Do you play yourself?"

"Sadly no, at least not for a while, but I used to be not bad as a boy."

"Ah well, in that case you've probably got a good swing. Look — when we get to Livorno I'm going to play a course in Tuscany. Why don't you come along and have a few holes. Don't worry about equipment. The course I'm going to is a resort setup that caters to Japanese and they have everything you need including shoes."

Jack had been wondering what to do about Livorno, which is the port for Florence. The key to enjoying Florence was timing. Like Venice it was mobbed in the summer, and he had been thinking that if he did go he would lunch as usual in a little family restaurant off the beaten track. But why not save Florence for another time? Why not golf?

"You're on, Robin. Let's do it. I'm going to make a complete ass of myself, I know, but I need the exercise."

CHAPTER 33

There are some wonderful cities such as Sydney or Vancouver where a big ship can sail right into the center, tie up, and passengers can come and go as if they were staying at the most central hotel, which indeed they are. Sadly Florence does not qualify, and cruise ships have to use the decidedly commercial — and ugly — port of Livorno, then go by road or rail to Florence.

Cathy had been all set to take the train because it was cheaper, and also because she thought it would have been an adventure, but Nick had told her of an experience of one of the crew. He, like everyone else, wanted to see the statue of David by Michelangelo, but when he arrived he found crowds lined up around the block in both directions. There was a three-hour wait. Just then he recognized people going through an entrance reserved for groups — and they were from his ship.

Cathy headed to the ship's shore excursion office and studied the tours to Florence, finding out in a moment that there was a tour that included the gallery where David was located, and yes, it came with timed tickets to get in. In other words, no waiting.

At the appointed hour Cathy disembarked the ship at Livorno, found the "Florence Highlights" tour bus waiting on the dock, and made her way to a seat at the back. A place at the front of the bus was out of the question as all the front seats had been grabbed by seniors who had got off the ship well before the scheduled departure time.

It reminded her of the story of the aircraft that was about to take off from Los Angeles when one of the crew noticed a young woman in a seat in first class that should have been vacant. When the passenger's ticket was checked it was for economy, but she said, "I'm blonde and pretty and I'm staying in first class all the way to New York."

Other cabin staff asked her to move but she simply repeated the same statement.

Finally the captain went to talk to her, after which she immediately got up and went to the back of the aircraft. The purser was delighted but could not resist asking the captain what he had said to the young woman. Said the captain, "Oh, I just told her that the front of the aircraft was not going to New York."

The trip to Florence was free of any such dramas, although Paulo the driver never stopped talking in a bid to endear himself to the company and earn tips. The story he told was pure fiction: that he had nine children, one of them handicapped.

The bus dropped the group in the middle of town, where a guide with a red and white umbrella met them. It was important, she said, to remain close to her, and to look out for pickpockets. Off they went, filing into museums and galleries, and in the process seeing two statues of David. Just one, however, was the original, and that was the statue indoors.

The other was outside, in a fine square with many antiquities to enjoy, and a sea of people flowing in and out. They included a group of children not there for the culture. Cathy instinctively pulled her handbag close to her chest when she saw them; just as well, for a group of four went to an elderly tourist wearing a pouch around his waist. One child of about 10 pushed a map into the man's belly as if asking for directions, after which a tiny urchin, unseen by the victim, ducked under the map and opened the pouch. It was over in a moment, and the tourist had lost $400 cash, credit cards, as well as his passport.

Cathy called out but even as the children ran away the tourist had no idea he had been robbed. One hour later Cathy crossed the square again and the children were back. She pointed them out to the guide who shrugged her shoulders. "The tourists make it easy for them, for example by wearing these stupid pouches which are an invitation to robbery. My sister sat at that café one day and watched children robbing tourists one after another. It was a production line."

There was a little time before the bus left Florence so Cathy bought postcards and sat at a café. She found the mailing address for Tom's camp and wrote, "This is a place so beautiful, so magical, so historical, I cannot start to do it justice. Just promise me that one day you will come here. With luck, I'll come back with you. Pray for your Dad."

She looked across the road at a majestic building of the Renaissance. Even the café had stones weathered by centuries and sported gargoyles watching over her. Whose horse had drunk at the trough in front of her — a Roman general's? And had legions tramped along this cobbled road?

Oh that Tom was here to share her fantasies. And Doc. Even Nick or Jack, she found herself thinking with an aftertaste of guilt. Her mind went back to a recurring thought that being in special places was only worthwhile if you have someone to share the experience. She recalled visiting an island off Seattle with two women friends, and when one of them remarked, "look at that sunset, isn't if romantic?" the other said, "Yeah, all we need now is the romance."

CHAPTER 34

Dinner on the ship that night was a jolly affair with Jack and Robin regaling Cathy and Diane with stories of their golfing day. The course would never hold the Italian Open, but it was quite acceptable for cruise passengers. The management had been accommodating and Robin was off to a good start.

"Another three or four courses like that," said Robin, "and the cruise line can offer a golf package. Let's have a drink to that."

"Count me in," said Jack, raising his glass with one hand and patting Robin on the back with the other, "I think Robin's got a great idea. As you'll gather I enjoyed my day even although I played like a complete idiot, but I'm going to try it again for a variety of reasons. One is that I need the exercise; secondly I've got the nauseating problem of having been everywhere and need a new take on ports of call. In future, instead of hanging around museums and then going for big lunches I'll play a round of golf ..."

"And then go for lunch," added Robin.

"Well maybe, but at least I'll have had some exercise. Hey, when I started going on cruise ships I had no difficulty keeping my weight down…"

"How was that, Jack?" said Diane with a knowing look.

Jack looked her straight in the eye. "If you must know, Diane, I was banging headboards like there was no tomorrow. But now I'm a reformed character."

"You are? Sounds very boring." It was Mike Brown, who had arrived at their table with Nick and a trolley.

"Ladies and gentlemen," said Mike, "Nick and I have a special dessert tonight — crêpes Suzette. Would anyone like to try it?"

"Bravo!" said Cathy and the others cheered their approval.

It was a good flambé, made by Mike although Nick had set up everything in advance. "And for your further enjoyment tonight," said Mike, "we will be doing a midnight buffet in the new upper deck lounge, where there will be other treats to tempt you."

"Oh, I like the sound of that," said Diane, "what time does it start?"

And so to the upper deck lounge, where a band was playing. They found a table by a huge window and sat and watched the lights of Italy on shore. Cathy and Robin were soon on the dance floor while Jack and Diane talked to people at the next table. One of them was a woman Jack had met on a previous cruise, and he introduced her to Diane, then suddenly jumped to his feet.

"Betty, how nice to see you!" exclaimed Jack. "Diane, this is Betty Brown, public relations manager for the cruise line. Hey Betty, I didn't know you would be here."

"It was a last-minute decision when a few cabins became available. Now I'll be able to give you a proper press tour of the ship, make sure you see the galley, the bridge, meet the hotel manager, make sure you miss none of the features of our five-star ship ..."

"I can't handle all this excitement!" said Jack with mock alarm.

"Okay, relax. But have you had a good look around our new ship? What do you think? I mean, isn't this a great night-time spot for example?"

"Just a bit over the top," said a woman at the next table.

"Tell me," asked Jack

"I was just in the ladies' washroom and one of the bartenders was having sex with a passenger."

"That's another thing," said Betty, "the service is *very* good."

CHAPTER 35

Ocean Odyssey arrived at Portofino at dawn. Cathy was wakened by the sound of the ship's anchor chain rattling off the foredeck. She lay in bed and pictured the ship swinging before the wind, the captain picking out a mark on shore and checking to see if the anchor had a solid grip.

Something was moving — well, the ship of course, Cathy realized, and with it a vertical slice of light, framed by her slightly open curtains, suddenly appeared on a wall of the cabin and slipped to the right, ever so slowly, then stopped on the door.

At that her doorbell rang.

Cathy jumped out of bed, her daydreaming over, put on her robe, and found Dan with her morning tea.

"Sorry to trouble you, Dan. I don't normally have room service in the morning but I didn't want to miss anything of Portofino."

"No problem. I am happy to be your wake-up call every day." Dan came in and put down the tray.

"Can I get you anything else?"

"No thanks. But you can tell me more about your not getting another contract. I think you are doing a very good job and can't imagine why the chief stewardess won't have you back."

Dan's eyes welled up with tears. "It's very complicated. She does not do the actual hiring but she has to make a recommendation to the head office, and she won't do that unless I pay her."

"You pay her?" exclaimed Cathy.

"I can't believe I am telling you this but what have I got to lose? Yes, she wants $400 to recommend me, which is what I have paid her before, and what the others give her. It's one month's pay before tips, and for many of the young staff, they can afford it. But I can't because of my responsibilities at home, and that's why I have to try to get a job with another company where I can make the money I need."

"But that's absurd!" said Cathy. "The woman is evil." And then she recalled seeing the chief stewardess in the Cartier shop in Sorrento.

"Dan, leave this to me. Madam Anna will walk the plank before we sail much farther." She put her arm around Dan and guided him to the door. "Don't worry about this. Say nothing, and leave it to me."

Dan made to protest but Cathy pushed him out of the door. "Bitch" she said under her breath.

She had a shower, dressed quickly and went up on deck. Portofino lay before her, a tiny harbor with a palette of pastel-colored houses wrapped around the shore, and behind them a wooded cliff dotted with handsome villas.

Cathy stood at the rail, taking in the prettiest picture in the Mediterranean, when Robin came by. He nudged her and said, "Smashing, isn't it? No artist could imagine, could create, anything to cap that."

"Hi Robin, yes, you're right. It's beautiful, and look at that majestic building high on the cliff. Is that a hotel?"

"It is indeed. That's the Hotel Splendido, where every movie star from Elizabeth Taylor to Humphrey Bogart has taken a suite, oh aye, and the new current heartthrobs as well. Anyway, you get the idea — it's right swanky."

"Robin, I gather you're not a movie fan?"

"You're right. Last good picture I saw was *Casablanca*. There's been nobody since to match Bogie. His picture's on the wall of the bar at the Splendido. I'll take you up there for a drink if you like. We could go after dinner."

"Not a bad idea, but I haven't had breakfast yet — I'm going to the stern café. You too?"

"Sounds good. Lead on, MacDuff."

They sat outside at the ship's rail with a panoramic view of Portofino. A waiter was with them in a flash. "Coffee, sir?" a smiling Filipino asked Robin.

"Two things, pal," said Robin. "You serve the lady first, and secondly, what did I tell your buddy yesterday before I pushed him over the side?"

The waiter could see that Robin was smiling, so he was not alarmed, but something was wrong.

"I'm not American. They are lovely people, but I'm different. I don't start my day with a swill of coffee that's been sitting in a pot since you guys dragged your backsides up here. I, like most British people, start my breakfast with orange juice.

So please bring me that — and the menu."

"Don't go away," said Cathy to the waiter. "I'm one of those Americans with no taste. I'd like a cup of that coffee."

When the waiter had left Robin said, "Sorry about that. It's all because of the incident with the captain's daughter. I can't walk a step around the ship without somebody chucking a red carpet in front of me."

Cathy laughed. "You were talking about Americans being lovely people. Well, we do have hearts of gold, but I must defer to those Filipino crew members. They are the best. They work hard, they smile … but there is something I must tell you."

CHAPTER 36

As they breakfasted Cathy explained to Robin about her steward Dan and the chief stewardess.

"Tricky one, that."

"Why?" asked Cathy. "Can't someone simply report it to the hotel manager or the captain?"

"You're right. But Anna, as she is called I gather, would be badly missed by half the senior officers starting with the chief engineer."

"How do you mean?"

"According to the gossip I hear — men's talk, you understand — she's a raver. Apparently she's the best thing in bed since Catherine the Great, and she bestows her favors around the ship to those in positions of power."

"I see. And do you suppose those grateful wretches who sleep with her have any idea what a thieving, despicable woman she is?"

"They may, or they may not. I really don't know."

"You talk as if you've been knocking on her door," said Cathy, looking Robin in the eye.

"No way, Jose, she's not my type. You are."

Cathy blushed.

"Look, I know your story and I don't want to embarrass you. I just want to say you are a wee stotter, and when I'm with you my heart soars and I don't even think about golf …"

"Oh stop it!" Cathy put her hand on his, then leaned across the table and kissed him on the cheek. "See you — and I can do a Scottish accent as well — you're getting salt water in your heid which is drowning your better senses. No man in his right mind should be bothering with a woman who has a husband, who lives for a letter in the mail that might say she can get on with her life. One day I might have to call it a day but not yet."

Robin put a finger under Cathy's chin, lifted her head so his eyes were looking into hers and said, "Forget what I said. We're pals, that's all."

Cathy was going to say something else when there was a public announcement from the bridge to say the ship had been cleared by local authorities and passengers could go ashore by tender.

At that moment Jack Silver came by. "Well, well, what are you guys up to today?"

"We were hoping you could point us in the right direction," said Cathy.

Jack explained he was going ashore for a coffee, to buy a newspaper, and then would take the local ferry to the next port, Santa Margarita. This idea met with approval, so Jack led the way. "Just beware," he said, "that the coffee in Portofino is going to be almost as expensive as Venice."

Jack was right. But at least it was good coffee. The threesome sat at a table and looked around at the stunningly beautiful little harbor, little wooden fishing boats at anchor, and a line of extravagant gin palaces docked stern-on to the old stone dock.

"So who's going up to the Hotel Splendido tonight?" asked Jack.

"We are," chorused Cathy and Robin.

"In that case, I have no option but to say you are complete idiots, but I will join you all the same. Can I recommend that we just have drinks? The dinner is to be recommended but I may have to sell my gold watch to pay for it. Then there's the matter of the wine…"

"Dinna fash yersel," said Robin, "which is Scottish for have no fear, we're just going for a drink as well."

"Good," said Jack, "but I do recommend a jacket and tie. Now, if you're ready to proceed with Silver's exclusive shore excursion, I see the harbor shuttle is about to leave."

CHAPTER 37

Days ashore around the Mediterranean usually center on lunch, and this was no exception. Jack did the ordering — bruschetta, fish landed that morning by the proprietor's son, and bottles of pinot grigio. They had a toast to "absent friends" and Cathy mouthed "to Doc."

"Your glass is empty, Cathy," said Robin, and another splash of the fruity young wine came her way. And why not — it was a day to celebrate the simple state of being alive. The sun was shining; there were palm trees, gingerbread buildings, and an azure sea.

When they got back to the ship Cathy found a note from Nick. He had some time off during the day when the ship was in Barcelona, and in the meantime what about tonight? He had to work but could meet her when the ship sailed.

She saw him at dinner as usual, then hurried off with Jack and Robin.

"Don't forget the last tender's at 11 PM," said the security man at the gangway.

"I'll be lucky if my money lasts till then," said Jack.

They chugged ashore, walked across the harbor plaza and found a hotel shuttle waiting. The hotel terrace had dramatic views, but they opted for the bar. "There's Bogie," said Robin, pointing out a black and white photograph on the wall.

"Too bad he's holding a cigarette," said Jack. "The Lucky Strikes got him at early age."

Robin raised his glass, "Did I ever tell you I have another hero — Blackbeard the pirate. He used to drink rum laced with gunpowder and he liked to say: *Give me a short life but a merry one!*"

"On that note," said Jack, "whose round is it?"

A jolly evening was passed in the elegant bar of the Hotel Splendido. The pianist played, they met a honeymoon couple off a private yacht in the harbor, and then the bill arrived.

"Have we bought the place?" said Robin.

"Told you," said Jack.

"Let's split it," said Cathy.

"Good idea," said the men.

And so they went back to the ship and said their goodnights.

Cathy went to her cabin, put her bag on the bed, combed her hair, and headed out again. Four decks down, at an aft area where ropes were piled high and passengers rarely ventured, she met Nick and fell into his arms.

Then they were kissing, a friendly greeting at first and then impulsively with a burst of passion, and their arms were around each other and her body was against his, and then he pulled away and held her head back.

His eyes burned with desire.

"Thank you for doing that. Now we must stop before we set the ship on fire."

"You don't mind?"

"I loved it. Do it again," and with that she threw her arms around Nick and kissed him as if there was no tomorrow. "Nick — give me time. As for today I've had to much wine to be in control."

Nick motioned her to a pile of ropes where they sat down. "Anything you say, Cathy, but if I may say so you kiss like a woman …"

"… who has not been kissed for a long time," interjected Cathy. "You're right — this girl has been living like a nun for many years, maybe too many."

"Cathy, don't let me spoil anything. I know that finding your husband is the most important thing in your life, and that …"

"… and that you don't want to lead me astray. Don't worry Nick. I am in control of that situation, or I thought I was until 10 minutes ago, and if anything changes, which it might, you will be the first to know …" and at that she put both her arms around his neck and kissed him tenderly, then long and hard like a teenager after the school dance.

"Wow," said Nick afterwards, "the ship moved."

"You rat," said Cathy with a smile, "I've read Hemingway. And anyway, you're getting ahead of yourself."

They watched the lights of Portofino slip astern, and Cathy went to bed, to dream.

CHAPTER 38

The next morning *Ocean Odyssey* was sailing along the French Riviera, past Monaco with its handsome wedding cake casino, and Nice and Cannes — all names to stir the imagination.

"So why are we stopping at St Tropez?" Diane asked Tony as he stepped out of her shower.

"You don't know St Tropez?"

"No I don't, but I sure heard of Monte Carlo. Didn't Grace Kelly marry the king?"

"She married Prince Rainier," said Tony, who finished drying himself and then hung his wet towel on the end of his erect penis.

"What are you doing, darling?"

"Demonstrating that I enjoy being with you, particularly when you are lying naked on the bed."

"Come to think of it, I did read that in Australia real men do it with two towels."

"On a good day maybe, but not after making love all night."

"Are we tired, darling?"

"Fucking exhausted. And now I have to go to work."

Tony got dressed quickly, looked through the spy-hole in the door to see if the coast was clear, blew her a kiss, and bolted across the corridor.

Jack Silver looked at the coast as he had breakfast on deck. He knew it well, and smiled to himself as he thought of his first flight into Nice airport, then the helicopter ride along the Riviera to Monte Carlo. He had been invited for dinner at the Hotel de Paris, the legendary restaurant frequented by stars and royalty, so he brought his dinner jacket, which he always called his penguin suit.

He was not alone — half the patrons were in dinner jackets, and so were the waiters, which had Jack wondering if anyone was ever flagged down by another customer and asked to bring the ketchup.

He soon began to enjoy Monte Carlo and its classic Belle Epoque buildings. The people he met were well traveled and apparently successful, mostly entrepreneurs who had made their fortunes and then parked their money in banks here or in some other tax haven. Monte Carlo had made a deal with France so that French people were forbidden to use the banks here, but there were many British, German, and other nationalities.

Not for nothing had Monte Carlo had been described by Somerset Maugham as a sunny place for shady people.

Nice and Cannes, on the other hand, were full of dull, middle-class French, mostly stacked like sardines in tiny apartments, whose cars clogged the narrow streets. Regardless of the war, a large number were German-made, such as the Mercedes favored by French butchers.

Then there was St Tropez. Now that was a place …

"Jack, you're miles away? Dreaming about someone?"

Jack looked up. Cathy wore a low-cut bathing wrap tied in the middle that just covered her thighs. She wore sandals with high heels and sunglasses on top of her head, and a smile that could have lit up Monte Carlo's casino.

"You've changed."

"Changed? You mean into my playsuit. You like it?"

"Yes I do, it's perfect for St Tropez. But that's not what I was meaning. Here — sit down, please join me."

A waiter came from nowhere and pulled out a chair. Cathy sat down, crossed her legs, and said, "Don't tell anyone, but I've had a sex-change operation. I thought I'd beat you to it."

"There you go," said Jack. "You wouldn't have talked like that when I met you. And you do look different — it's not just what you are wearing, although I must say you could stop the traffic on the Promenade des Anglais, but something has happened. Have you met a man?"

"Have I met a man? You bet — I've met at least three in the last little while, and you're one of them. But as you would say," and here Cathy put her hand on Jack's knee, "we have not exactly been banging headboards, have we?"

"There you go again," said Jack with a smile, "talking like a scarlet woman. Hey, don't get me wrong, I'm not complaining. I'd just like some of the action that has put you in this alluring frame of mind."

Cathy lowered her voice and squeezed Jack's knee. "Yeah right, what about your being gay?"

"That was yesterday," laughed Jack. "You have put me back on the straight and narrow."

"Enough of this nonsense. I am a respectable married woman who has acquired an affection for cruise ships, and part of that allure, to use your word, is the fact I have met a certain number of attractive men with whom I have become friendly ... but that's the extent of it. So there, Jack Silver. Now, when do we arrive in St Tropez?"

"In two hours. We have to tender ashore, we overnight here, and sail at six tomorrow evening. It's a fun place. Come with me tomorrow and wear exactly what you have on now."

"We're going to the beach?"

"We are — to the best beach club in the world."

Cathy put her head on the pillow and thought about Jack's remarks and wondered if he was right. Maybe he was, maybe a fire had started somewhere. Whatever it was, she was enjoying the glow. Surely to feel so good, so warm inside, was not wrong? Was it not just a matter of containing the flames until she knew some answers? Sleep consumed her as the ship rocked gently at anchor.

CHAPTER 39

St Trop, as it's known, lies just west of Cannes and Nice and is considerably smaller than its neighbors. There is a picturesque little harbor not unlike Portofino, also lined with extravagant yachts, and a waterfront with cafes, restaurants and boutiques. Just behind, there is a maze of narrow streets and a dirt-covered square where men play boules under the shade of olive trees, except when the market comes to town.

Celebrities starting with Brigitte Bardot and rocker Johnny Hallyday are easily spotted here, if not in the bars, restaurants and nightclubs, then on the beach, miles of golden sand lapped by the warm Mediterranean.

It was a bold move by the cruise line to come here because St Tropez is less well known to Americans than Cannes or Nice. But some well-traveled person in the shore excursion department thought they would try St Tropez because it had good shopping (always a winner) and a day on a beach would be a change.

Jack Silver could not agree more. He liked to stroll the waterfront where painters strained to perfect light on water in a salty version of Monet, he loved to see the beautiful young women who are drawn to St Tropez like moths to a candle, and then there were the smells — of fish on the dock, pastis in the bars and fresh baguettes in the shops.

St Tropez, in Jack's book, was special, although preferably not in August when most of France, and definitely Paris, was on holiday.

The ship's tender nosed into St Tropez harbor, squeezing past fishing boats, sailing boats and gleaming yachts. At the quayside there was just room between the easels of two painters for the passengers to squeeze through. Cathy, who led the way, was about to apologize to the closest one for the interruption, when she saw he was doing a quick sketch of a tourist. The artist smiled; with this traffic it would be a good day.

Jack and Robin followed and they all went for a stroll, then had coffee at a waterfront café.

"Right," said Robin, "I'm off to St Maxime for the golf. I'm being picked up right over there in five minutes. See you guys later."

Jack and Cathy lingered for a while, enjoying the passing parade of tourists who in turn were gawking at the yachts docked stern-on just a few feet from their stares. Every so often an under-dressed man or woman would appear on deck then realize it was like stepping out the front door of their home into a street of strangers. The old hands were more circumspect, but St Tropez always had its share of the nouveau riche who chartered a yacht in the hope of fitting in with the rich and famous.

"Is that what the British call the filthy rich?" asked Cathy.

"Well, I wouldn't say they are poor, but the real money is in villas along the beach, or in bigger boats that can't get in here." Jack looked at his watch. "Time to go."

It was noon at Club 55 when Jack and Cathy arrived by taxi. A young man immaculate in white shirt and shorts led them to the beach where Jack had reserved two loungers under a simple wooden shelter.

Cathy looked around for a place to change and saw what looked like a small house behind and showers to the right. She went up the beach, found a changing cubicle and put on a bikini.

When she got back, Jack was stretched out on his lounger with a smile as wide as the *Herald Tribune* that lay by his side.

"So whatdya think of this place?"

"If you really want to know, I think I'm overdressed."

Jack looked around and two other sunbathing women were both topless, while another emerging from the water was covered by the merest strip of a bikini bottom.

"Well, this is the Riviera," said Jack. "Actually this place is quite discreet — peek over that fence to the left and you'll see the naked bodies of German campers, and it's not always a pretty sight.

"Things were different before. See this stretch of beach …" and Jack waved his hand to the right. "This is where the American Army arrived in 1944 when liberating southern France. Then in 1955 Brigitte Bardot came here.

If the GIs had known she was on her way they'd never have left. Anyway Brigitte made her first big movie right here — *And God Created Woman*. It was a sensation and launched her as a sex symbol idolized by every Frenchman, not to mention over-excited men everywhere else.

"See that little house behind us — the people living there made meals for the film crew, and they did it so well they decided to stay in business when the movie was completed. They called it Club 55.

"Over the years they added the beach chairs and the shop, and for my money it's the best on the Riviera. Oh there are others, but they are mostly bigger and flashier. Club 55 looks insignificant from the road but wait till you see the restaurant and the customers. The valet parking kid gets to drive better cars than the staff at the Hotel de Paris in Monte Carlo, and as for that big yacht out there — and Jack nodded to a whopper dropping anchor offshore — the owner will be coming ashore with his guests, assuming he has made his reservation well in advance."

"In that case I'm not likely to bump into anyone from the office here," said Cathy, reaching behind her back to undo her bikini top. Tossing the piece of cotton on her lounger and picking up a bathing cap, Cathy walked 20 yards to the calm, azure sea and felt the temperature with her right foot. It was perfect. She put on the cap backwards, tucked in her hair, then slipped in the sea and swam with a powerful stroke.

Perhaps because she was from a city by the sea, perhaps because she was far from home, or perhaps simply because she was not in the confines of a pool, Cathy felt energy and strength flowing into her strokes. Kicking hard and scything the water with reaching fingertips, her crawl left a track like a torpedo.

On and on she raced, reveling in the freedom of being almost naked, leaving the coast behind and with nothing ahead but Africa.

Africa! Not today, and she made a swift turn, looking up at the same time. Just as well, for a motorboat was not far away, and she could see it had a driver in a peaked cap and several people in the back. One, a man with striking blond hair, waved and called to her, "Lovely day for a dip."

Cathy waved and struck out for the shore. The motorboat, a classic, mahogany Riva, continued on its stately way.

Back on the beach Jack put aside his *Herald Tribune* and looked up. Cathy's return, he allowed, was worthy of any James Bond movie, and when she took off her cap and shook her hair every male heart at Club 55 missed a beat.

"Enjoy that?" asked Jack.

"Wonderful. I felt so free. I think I'll be a mermaid in my next life."

Cathy pulled her lounger into the sun and lay down. "Don't let me burn for more than 15 minutes on either side."

"Will do. Sweet dreams."

Cathy lay on her stomach and tasted the salt water on her lips. The last time she had swum in the sea had been with Doc when they were with friends on a sailboat in the San Juan Islands off Seattle. It seemed so long ago, so far away.

Jack's hand on her arm made her wake up. "I wouldn't bother with the other side — this sun is hot. Another five minutes and the locals will be saying you are a *rosbeef* like the British. And on that note, let's do lunch."

Cathy went for a shower and got dressed. Then they went to the restaurant. It was surprisingly big, or maybe just very busy, or both, bubbling with conversation, all eyes on every entrance, and although many famous faces did come to Club 55 it was mostly regulars.

The menu was simple, the food perfect. Cathy had a salad with prawns and Jack a fish cooked in Pernod. Their wine was a rosé from Provence and the warm bread had been freshly baked. As for the atmosphere it was refreshingly cool, thanks to occasional bursts of chilled water finely sprayed from overhead pipes.

"I like this place," said Jack. "Look at that couple over there — the pretty young girl and the older man. Bet you anything that's not his daughter. I'd say he has a big heart — or a big wallet."

"Oh Jack, you're such a cynic." She looked around and saw the blond man who had been in the motorboat when she was swimming. He saw her too and raised his glass in a toast.

"Found a new friend?" asked Jack. "I just happen to know him — it's Chris Vernon, and he is a top Wall Street broker, a man with the Midas touch."

"Good for him," said Cathy, turning back to face Jack. "Let me say that I am more than happy with my companion today. Thank you, Jack, for bringing me here."

"Pleasure's all mine — now let's get back to the beach. You've got some sun to catch up with — can't have you brown on one side and white on the other."

Jack ushered Cathy ahead of him as they made their way out. Heads turned to look at Cathy, and it was really no surprise when a voice called out, "Jack — over here!"

It was Chris Vernon. Jack touched Cathy on the arm and led her over to his table. Chris Vernon jumped to his feet and pumped Jack's hand. "How are you doing, you old rascal?"

"Cathy — this is Chris Vernon. We have met on cruises once or twice. But that was a while back. He's now so rich he has his own boat."

Chris Vernon took her hand. "We almost met before lunch but you were going full throttle for Africa."

"I was, then I remembered our lunch was in St Tropez and not in Tunis."

"Are you planning any other Mediterranean crossings while you are here?"

"You never know — Jack and I are on a cruise ship heading for Barcelona and Malaga, and if we keep eating at the same rate I may be tempted to take some major swims just to keep in shape."

"If I may say so you are doing a very good job. Take a look around — you have made quite an impression in this restaurant, a place that is not easily impressed."

"You're very kind. Now, if you'll excuse us, we are going back to the beach."

"Before you go — how rude of me," said Chris Vernon, "please meet my friends. "This is Tony, Anne, Roger and Juliet."

Cathy nodded to the group.

"Who knows, we may bump into you again. What ship are you on?"

"*Ocean Odyssey*," said Jack. "Here's my card with my cell phone number on it. Give me a call — I'd love to see your gin palace."

"That I will do. Goodbye to you both, and fair winds."

Chris Vernon shook Jack's hand, then turned to Cathy. His handshake was the gentle affection of a smitten man.

Back on the ship Cathy found a letter in the mail-clip on her door. It was an invitation — to have dinner the following evening with the chief engineer.

I wonder, she thought. I wonder …

She phoned the RSVP number on the card and said she would be there.

CHAPTER 40

The next day *Ocean Odyssey* was at sea. Cathy had her hair done, had a massage, returned her book to the library, wrote postcards to Tom and Doc as well as the gang at the office, and still had time to sit on the deck.

"Lovely to watch the world go by," said the woman in the next lounger.

"It sure is," said Cathy.

"You a regular cruiser?"

"Not really, my second trip only."

"My first, and I can't believe the great service we get on this ship. Everyone is so kind — the waiters, my steward, and of course the dance hosts. They're real gentlemen."

"So you're having a good time?"

"Too right I am. But one thing upsets me. My steward is having to get off in Barcelona, and he tells me it's because his boss wants money from him to renew his contract. Is that normal on a ship?"

"Is that right?" said Cathy. "No I don't think it is normal. Can I ask your name and cabin number, and the name of your steward?"

The woman gave her the information, and said the steward was Pepe.

It was the last formal night of the cruise and the ship was awash with sequins. Men too made an effort, with most of them in dinner jackets. Standing out and looking quite resplendent were the ship's officers in their tight-fitting trousers, starched white shirts, and short jackets the British called bum freezers. The chief welcomed his guests who included Cathy, Jack, a couple from Australia, two single women from California, and Anna, the chief stewardess.

It was immediately clear that Anna had not held back when the aperitifs were going around, and when the wine steward arrived and poured her a glass of white Burgundy, she threw it back like a gunfighter in a salon.

The chief, who was sitting opposite to Anna, shifted uncomfortably in his seat. It was going to be one of those nights.

The Australians, who were not exactly sober either, flagged over the waiter. "Got any Oz wine, mate?" asked the male specimen.

"We do indeed, and that's what the chief has selected for tonight - a pinot noir from South Australia."

"Good on you, mate. We'll have a good gargle of that."

The two American women, who did not drink, looked as if they would rather be in a cage with a particularly hungry lion.

The chief, being a cool Swede, decided to go with the flow, ordering caviar and a slug of ice-cold vodka.

This, thought Jack, is going to be quite a party.

As for Cathy, she thought it was shaping up nicely for a showdown with that rat Anna.

The food came, the wine flowed, and everyone had a jolly time except the two American women called Milly and Molly. They were not that old, but they had obviously not been out much. Neither had any interest in the ship's engines, and when the Australian man mentioned that Melbourne had almost as many Greeks as Athens, that did not spark any interest either. But there was one thing.

"I see we have to tip the waiter and steward," said Milly. "My waiter's been okay but my steward has been too kind. Can I give him more than the ship guide recommends?"

"What's his name?" interjected Anna.

"Dan."

"I wouldn't. He's not the greatest."

This was the moment. Cathy spoke so everyone at the table could hear, "Is that why you are asking Dan for $400 to renew his contract? And Pepe's too?"

"I don't know what you are talking about," said Anna, visibly reddening.

"I'm talking about your extorting money from young Filipinos on this ship."

"Rubbish. That's rubbish. I am paid a modest salary and I get by on that and nothing else."

"So modest that you were shopping for expensive watches in Sorrento. In fact is that not a Cartier on your wrist?"

Anna looked at the watch, at the Chief, then jumped to her feet and ran out of the dining room.

"Sorry about that," said Cathy to the Chief. "Sorry to have to do that."

The Chief bowed his head and said nothing.

The next morning Cathy was wakened by Dan with a cup of tea.

"Missy, you won't believe what has happened. My friend Pepe was supposed to get off today because his contract was not being renewed. Now he has been told he can stay — and the chief stewardess has gone. I just carried her bags down the gangway. That means I can stay as well."

That was the way things happened on ships. Punishment at dawn — just like walking the plank.

CHAPTER 41

Barcelona! The name rolls around the tongue like the rich, red wine of Tarragona. Cathy liked Barcelona immediately because it started right where the ship docked. Had she not read that the only way to approach a great city was by sea?

She and Nick walked from *Ocean Odyssey*'s berth near the old port to La Rambla and the statue of Christopher Columbus.

"He is a great hero of mine," said Nick. "Okay I am Greek but our day in the sun was a very long time ago. I can relate more to Columbus because he was one of the fathers of the modern world we live in. The riches that came to Spain had to pass through Seville and not Barcelona, or anywhere else for that matter, but some gold did come here. Farther up La Rambla you will see a splendid classical-baroque palace built in 1771 by Philip V's viceroy to Peru."

"You have done your homework, or maybe you were a conquistador in your former life?" said Cathy teasingly.

"Who knows, but I enjoy Spain — the people, the history, the wine. The food I'm not so sure about. They do fish very well but they use too much oil, and even the English do better vegetables."

"My, we are very opinionated today. I think I'm getting to know you better."

"You think so?" said Nick, taking her hand. "What else can I tell you?"

"Anything you like so long as it's about Barcelona," replied Cathy, squeezing his arm affectionately.

Nick led her up the tree-lined La Rambla, a two-kilometer walk to the Placa de Catalunya. They digressed to elegant squares, saw the opera house, the food market and several palaces. There were musicians, mime artists and tarot readers, flower stalls and cafés. They stopped at one for *dos café solo* and were entertained by a group of Americans at the next table relating their adventures on the Metro, or underground.

What happened was that one had his pocket picked by a thief just as they were getting off at a station. However, the theft was witnessed by a local Spaniard who snatched the wallet from the thief and threw it out the carriage door just as it was closing. The victim heard a shout and turned around to see his wallet landing at his feet — and the Good Samaritan giving him a cheerful wave.

Cathy checked her bag. Nick patted his wallet. All present and correct.

Forewarned, they set off again on the trail of Antoni Gaudi, the immensely talented Catalan architect who created art nouveau masterpieces such as the Sagrada Familia, Europe's most unconventional church and still unfinished, and Casa Mila, completed in 1910 and without a single straight wall inside.

Cathy and Nick lunched at an outdoor café at Placa Reial, Barcelona's most formal square, which has ornate lampposts designed by Gaudi.

The waiter brought two glasses of cava, Spain's sparkling wine. "Wonderful to have your company," said Nick, raising his glass.

"I'm here thanks to you, and I'm loving every minute of it."

As they chinked glasses the waiter brought a steaming platter of *graellada de marisc*, grilled seafood with garlic mayonnaise.

Scorning the pedestrian notion that white wine should be drunk with fish, they opted for a regional red wine, the hearty Tarragona.

"This is delicious," said Cathy.

"I must warn you that if you drink too much, as before, I may take advantage of you," said Nick with a mock leer on his face.

"More wine!"

Their laughter rolled across the old flagstones of the placa.

CHAPTER 42

The last night was quiet, which was the way Cathy wanted it. She dressed for dinner, choosing the same clothes she would be traveling in the next day, put a toilet bag and change of underwear in a carry-on flight bag, closed her suitcases, and put them outside the cabin door for collection. Then she saw her steward.

"Dan! I've been looking for you."

She led him into the cabin and closed the door. "How are things — are you staying on board?"

"Yes, thanks to you. Pepe as well, and several others. The chief stewardess was a bad woman. We are all very grateful to you."

Cathy put her arm around his shoulder. "Think nothing of it — now here, put this to good use."

Dan took the envelope that contained his tip for the week. "This will be at my home in Manila within one week. Me and my family can't thank you enough."

At that her phone rang and Dan backed out with a wave. It was Jack. He was having a farewell drink with

Robin and the captain. Two minutes later Cathy walked into the bar and all the men jumped to their feet. Captain Criticos kissed her on both cheeks, ordered champagne, and when it came toasted Robin once again as the bravest man in the Adriatic, the Mediterranean and maybe all the seven seas.

"Whew!" said Robin when the captain had left, "I can imagine where he's coming from, but see me, another week on this ship and I'd be an alcoholic. You know what arrived in my cabin today? A bottle of Metaxa — another one! I could just about float the ship on the stuff."

Dinner was a little subdued, particularly for Cathy and Robin. He was not sure if he would see her again, but they made light of it as people do. "Keep in touch," he said, giving Cathy his address. He was also getting off in Malaga but staying in the Costa del Sol region to check out golf courses.

Diane was in fine form. She'd had a week of torrid horizontal entertainment with Tony but was now looking forward to going home. "Now I just have to finish my packing. You know on my last cruise I put all my clothes in my suitcase, put it outside and went to bed. Well, in the morning I had nothing to wear — had to go ashore in my bathrobe and root around in the customs hall for my bags and I tell you in was a nightmare…"

Soon after the ship arrived at Malaga, Nick came to her cabin. On Disembarkation Day a ship is swarming with people and crew can go more or less where they want.

He closed the door and put his arms around her. They kissed. "Goodbye, take care of yourself, and let's do this again."

Cathy held his hands. "I'd like to, very much. Now go — before I change my mind and stay on the ship."

Nick kissed her lightly on the cheek and walked out of the cabin without looking back. It was hard to do, but this woman was special, and she was not to be rushed. He would wait.

CHAPTER 43

Seattle welcomed Cathy home with clouds and rain and the flight was an hour late, but her spirits lifted when she saw Shirley in the arrivals area.

"Good to see you," said Cathy, throwing her arms around Shirley. "You are my ray of sunshine."

"Don't mention it. I wish. The weather has been awful since you left." Shirley steered Cathy's luggage trolley towards the terminal door and they made a dash for Shirley's car. On the way home Cathy said, "It was a wonderful cruise. I loved the ship, the places we went, the people I met…"

"Ah yes," said Shirley, "and how was your friend?"

"Fine, just fine," said Cathy nonchalantly. "He was just one of several people I met."

"I'm not asking any more questions," said Shirley, putting her hand on Cathy's arm. "I feel like I am prying."

"No, no — it's nothing like that. Cruising is very sociable."

"Yeah, I know — you're all in the same boat and all that."

"Yes — boat, not bed," said Cathy, turning to Shirley and they both laughed so loudly Shirley almost lost control of her car.

Cathy opened a bottle of wine when they got to her home. "You wouldn't believe what some women get up to on ships," she said, starting off with Diane's adventures with Tony. "Sure, I had the same opportunities. Heck, there were hundreds of young men on board, many of them Greeks who regard themselves as God's gift to women. Some of them I have gotten to know, and Nick, who I have told you about, is a lovely man. On this trip I also met a golf professional from Scotland who was great company, and there was a travel writer who had been on the Alaska cruise as well."

"My, you are going to be sending more Christmas cards this year."

"Absolutely. I may even have to buy a little black book."

They laughed again. It was good to be home.

Tom arrived the next day on the Boy Scouts' bus, and right on time.

Cathy hugged him until he squealed. "Mom — the other boys are looking."

"That's their problem. Their moms have not been on the other side of the world. And how come you are here just when I expected you, and yesterday my flight was an hour late? Maybe we need the Boy Scouts running the airline."

"Funny you said that. On the way back the Scoutmaster and his assistant were talking about one airline and they said it was a Mickey Mouse outfit. I would think we could do better than Mickey Mouse and those guys."

"I'm sure you could. Now come inside and tell me all about the jamboree."

Cathy looked at the laundry Tom had brought back. "Did you share the campsite with a herd of hippos?"

"Huh?"

"How come everything is caked in thick mud?"

"Dunno."

She tried another line of questioning. "When did you last have a shower?"

"Dunno."

"Well in that case get into the shower before the public health authorities come and take us away. Now!"

Tom reappeared in 10 minutes with a towel around his waist and another load of washing. "My, Puget Sound will be mucky today. You'd better warn the Navy to keep its subs on the surface."

"Mom! It's not as bad as that. Mom … have you heard anything about Dad?"

"No, I'm sorry, I have not. I have checked the mail and nothing came in our absence."

"Mom … at the jamboree I heard a Scoutmaster say he had read in a newspaper that the Vietnamese government still have American prisoners-of-war."

Cathy's heart missed a beat. "You did? I'll check that out. Now you go and get dressed, and let me know if you have everything you need for school going back in two days."

She picked up the phone and dialed the Navy in Washington, DC.

"Intelligence, please."

"Can I help you ma'am?"

"My name is Robertson. My husband is MIA."

She got through to a man called Fleming she had talked to in the past. She asked him about the newspaper report.

"We saw that, and there continue to be unconfirmed reports that POWs are still being held, for what reason we don't know, but I will say this — there are signs the government wants to normalize relations with Washington and in that event Hanoi must come clean about POWs. When we hear anything we will of course let you know right away."

Cathy hung up the phone. She had heard it all before. Reports and rumors, denials and disappointments. It was a depressing circle of events. She felt tears coming and went into the bedroom to get a tissue. Damn the war, damn the Navy, damn the government in Hanoi, she thought. The war's over, so why can't someone simply say if my husband is dead or alive? And if he is alive, why don't they send him home? Then she collapsed on her bed, sobbing.

Tomorrow was another day, and when she went to work she felt better. She also sought out Shirley, going into her office and shutting the door. "Who's that psychiatrist you were seeing?"

"You don't want to know."

"How come?"

"He's in jail."

"Jail?"

"Yeah — he was having sex with his patients. Well, most of them do that. But this guy got greedy and took advantage of a young girl."

"But, did he ..."

"Sure, he tried it on me but I knew all about him: that he was a good doctor but had lousy morals. His approach was to steer a woman patient to his couch, have sex with her, and say, 'Well, that's my problem solved — what's yours?' I think it helped that I worked for a newspaper."

"I'll give him a pass. Know anyone else?"

"Yup — his wife."

"No thanks, I think I'll deal with this myself."

"What's on your mind? Doc?"

"What else? I feel I'm getting close to a breaking point. I need to know, to move on. Heck, my subconscious is in overdrive. Last night I had a dream that I was with another man."

"Was he on a ship?"

"We were making love on top of the bridge and woke up the captain."

"Oh my God — no half measures. How did you get to be on top of the bridge?"

"I don't know, but if you've got sex on your mind you can get very creative on a cruise ship."

"Cathy — I think you're ready to move on."

"I know. That's what I've been thinking. There don't seem to be regulations about this but I gather that the wife of a serviceman missing for a year can request his reclassification as Killed in Action. But how can I do that? It would be like signing a death warrant."

Cathy knew it was not an option. Suppose Doc walked in the front door a week after she had ended their marriage — and signed away her son's father.

And she had heard of other wives in her situation who had done that in an attempt to find a form of closure. In one case the wife of a missing pilot remarried, got divorced, and was conveniently single again when her husband was freed.

CHAPTER 44

The following week she and Shirley went to the pub for a quiz night. Several others from the newspaper, including a new reporter called Richard Maxwell, were there as well, and six of them made up a team.

As the quiz neared its conclusion Cathy's team was neck and neck with the team at the next table. That team was asked if the Bahamas were in the Caribbean Sea or the Atlantic Ocean. The Caribbean, of course, one of them said.

No, said Cathy, the Atlantic.

And she was right. The newspaper team took first prize and won a round of drinks. Richard, who was sitting across from Cathy, raised his glass and said to her, "Not just a pretty face after all?"

"Not as green as I'm cabbage-looking, as my mother used to say," replied Cathy, raising her glass and chinking it with everyone else around the table.

On the way out Richard told Cathy he had an invitation for a restaurant opening the following Friday. It was a new venture by celebrated Vancouver restaurateur Umberto Menghi. Would she like to come?

Before she could stop herself she said yes. And when she did have time to think about it she did not change her mind. But it was not just Richard and his tall, good looks or the easy way he wore a chalk-striped suit, she just wanted to be out there.

Friday night could not come quickly enough for Cathy. She dug out her slinkiest little black dress, then put it back thinking that would send the wrong message. The aim was to say she was going to have a life, not that she had given up on her husband.

Even so, she was one of the most striking women at the party, and Umberto made a fuss over her when she arrived.

Then Donald Jones, the editor of the newspaper she worked for, came over. "Well, well — fancy seeing you here. I've never seen you at an event like this before. Richard — are you leading this woman astray?"

"Doing my best, sir."

"How was your trip to Europe?"

"If the truth be known," said Cathy confidentially, "I went on a cruise in the Med. But I didn't talk about it at the water fountain in case rumors started that I had run off with a sailor."

"Those things do happen."

"You mean running off with sailors? Not my style. I was exploring the magnificence of Venice, the glories of Florence ..."

"I see you resisted the waist-expanding splendor of the midnight buffet."

At that a waiter came by with canapés. Cathy took one, then helped herself to a glass of champagne from another tray.

"I did. Ship food is good, but this is better."

"Sounds like you are getting to know your way around. Are you planning another cruise?"

"Not saying," smiled Cathy.

"Well, good to see you here, and good luck," said Donald.

Good luck? Did he sense she was taking a different road?

Richard, in the best traditions of the press, hosed down four glasses of champagne, perhaps eight glasses of red wine, and tucked into the canapés and then the buffet. But he stayed on his feet, and he was good company, introducing Cathy to a Bohemian-looking man called Garth.

"Richard and I share a house," said Garth.

"Sounds cozy."

"Sometimes too cozy as Richard is actually the most untidy man in the world. He needs a wife."

"Don't look at me. I'm taken."

"Too bad. I was going to say Richard is a good cook and we like dinner parties. But before you panic I'm the washer-upper. We want you for your beauty and charm, not your skills in the kitchen."

Richard went by at that moment, steering a slightly tipsy blonde girl to the door. He looked over to Cathy and Garth and rolled his eyes.

"He'll be back in a moment," said Garth. "Richard won't put up with women who can't hold their booze. He's actually a very ethical guy. Maybe it comes from all the time he spends reporting crime cases from the courts."

Said Cathy, "Richard gives the impression that the closest he comes to crime is being slightly out of fashion."

Garth laughed. "How right you are."

Richard sauntered back into the room. "She works in public relations at the airport. I put her in a taxi. When she comes down to earth tomorrow she'll have a very sore head."

"You're a good man," said Cathy.

""Maybe one day she'll remember my chivalry."

"Stop it," smiled Cathy, "I have to go."

"I'll get your coat," said Richard.

"No, it's okay. You are having a good time here and I'm sure you have unfinished business. If you don't mind I'd rather leave on my own — I'm sure you understand why. But very many thanks for bringing me along. I appreciate it, a lot." She took his arm, pulled him down to her height, and kissed him lightly on the cheek.

She did the same to Garth, but only Richard was on her mind as she left. The feel of that chalk-stripe sleeve was quite sensuous, and as for the cologne he was wearing ... Cathy gulped the fresh air as she walked outside the restaurant.

CHAPTER 45

It was a few days later and Cathy was at work. Donald Jones came into her office and put the *New York Times* on her desk. "Seen that?"

Cathy followed his finger to a story about the body of an American airman being returned by Hanoi. He was an air force captain whose F105 Thunderchief had been shot down in 1972.

"Note the date," said Donald. "Same year Doc went missing, but only now are they admitting they have his remains. I think what is happening is that they are trying to normalize relations with Washington."

Donald put his hand on her shoulder. "There's more. Read on."

The article went on to say that an American transport aircraft had gone to Da Nang to pick up the body. While there one of the crew had been told that the air force captain had been held briefly in the Hanoi Hilton, but as he was injured he had been moved to a hospital where he died.

As for the Hanoi Hilton, the crewman was told, it did not hold any American POWs after April 1973.

Donald pulled up a chair. "One way or another your ordeal may be coming to an end. But don't fear the worst — there have been reports of work camps in remote parts of Vietnam. Heck, after the Second World War the Russians kept hundreds of thousands of German soldiers prisoner in the Soviet Union and put them to work for years. Many died in the salt mines of Siberia, but some did return eventually."

He looked at Cathy to see tears in her eyes. "Yes Donald, he might be alive, or he might be dead. I just want to know…" and her voice rose and then fell and her head collapsed into her hands.

When Cathy got home that night Tom met her at the door. "Hi Mom, you got mail." There was lots of it, bills mostly, but Cathy recognized a letter with Nick's handwriting. She put it aside to read after dinner.

"Right, rascal — how was school today?"

"Same old, same old. Mom, nothing ever changes at my school. It's the most boring place on the planet. But there is life beyond school — like at the Scouts. I have a meeting tonight at the Scout Hall. Sorry, I forgot to tell you. Can I get going in half an hour?

"You can, because your mother is a miracle worker and this here pasta will be ready in 10 minutes. Go get washed and changed and present yourself in the dining room in nine minutes — flat!"

Tom dashed off and Cathy busied herself in the kitchen.

Later she sat in a chair by the window and opened Nick's letter. It was short, as usual. Nick never got carried away with his correspondence but he always had something to say. He was being promoted again — to maître d' on the *Golden Odyssey*, the same ship where they had met on her first cruise to Alaska.

The *Golden Odyssey* would be in the Caribbean that winter doing a series of short cruises out of Ft. Lauderdale. Nick wrote, "Cathy dear, you must come and visit, if only to get the best table on the ship! Also I am going to be in America — so close to you!!"

Cathy came to a conclusion. Like the other wives, she needed closure — a time when the waiting ended. One year from this day and she would declare to herself that Doc was not coming home. After that she would get a new life.

Was she saying she would start dating men, perhaps sleeping with them? That she did not want to contemplate. What she was deciding was to not to compromise herself or Doc in the meantime. Maybe then she would talk to a lawyer and see if some kind of legal separation was possible. She winced at her choice of words. This was not a divorce, but if not, what was it?

Cathy looked out the window. She was searching for an answer that was not in this world; could the heavens help her? No, not in Seattle. It was overcast as usual, sealing off salvation from on high. She smiled to herself. What a pickle.

Could she tell anyone of her decision? Perhaps Shirley, perhaps not. Doc could come home one year and a day from now, so she would continue to keep her personal life beyond reproach.

Well, on dry land at least — had Jack Silver not said that the real world remained on the dock?

CHAPTER 46

Winter is not Seattle's best season. It never gets really cold but clouds hang overhead for weeks on end, casting gloom and often rain over the city. Those who can afford it hop on planes and fly to Hawaii, five hours away in the middle of the Pacific. Cathy knew Hawaii well, and always marveled that although many Americans took it for granted, not just as a state but as part of their backyard, Hawaii was in fact one of the most remote islands in the world. As one airline pilot asked her, think of another place that requires such a long flight over sea.

One winter weekend Cathy decided to take Tom on a little trip — not to Hawaii, but on a ship to Canada.

They took a ferry to Victoria on Vancouver Island. And not any ferry — but a fine old vessel called the *Princess Marguerite*, whose funnel was emblazoned with the British flag, a perfectly apt thing to do as Victoria is more British than Britain itself.

Tom was intrigued with the old ship. It had teak decks and brass fittings and lots of pictures of sister ships with glorious pedigrees, such as a namesake built on the River Clyde in Glasgow in 1925 for the Seattle-Vancouver run. When war came, the *Princess Marguerite* became a troopship and was sunk by a German submarine off the Egyptian coast.

Cathy and Tom's trip was but a few hours, but amazingly Seattle's drizzle had been left behind and Victoria greeted them with blue skies and sunshine. Cathy was on deck when Tom joined her. "This is a nice way to go, Mom. Is this the same as a cruise ship?"

"Sort of − it's relaxing, you can smell the sea and there's the gentle throb of the engines."

"I suppose the food's better on a cruise ship."

"Well, there's certainly more of it."

"I'll bet you enjoyed your cruise to Alaska. It must have been like this, the scenery I mean."

"It was, Tom. I was surprised myself, I can't think why, but the scenery around here, and just to the north in British Columbia is maybe prettier than Alaska − it's just that Alaska has more of it. Take a look over there."

Tom turned and behind them were the snow-capped Olympic Mountains. Cathy tapped him on the shoulder and pointed left. More mountains − this time the Coast Range of British Columbia with Whistler Mountain in the distance. They too were draped with snow. Tom whistled softy. "Hey Mom, this is a special place."

"It is Tom. You are a lucky young man to be living in a lively city yet so close to raw nature. There's bears in the mountains and whales in the sea…"

"Not now, Mom."

"Yes, I know, they come in the summer, but you know what I mean."

"What's that Mom?"

Just then the *Princess Marguerite* made a sharp turn round a point of land where a row of young women were waving. It was immediately clear they were not in any distress but were standing in front of a hotel, the Laurel Point. Wearing smart maids' outfits, the girls were welcoming the American day-trippers to Victoria. And for sure, many of the hundreds of passengers who waved back also asked, "What is that place?" — and went for lunch.

Cathy walked Tom around the harbor to the Empress Hotel, a beautiful old stone building that had welcomed kings, queens and presidents. What she did not tell him was that the architect, Rattenbury, was murdered by his chauffeur after the latter had an affair with his wife. I bet Jack Silver knows that story, thought Cathy with a laugh.

"What's so funny Mom?"

"Oh nothing, I was thinking about something far away. But Tom, you'll get a kick out of this place. Let's walk down the main street and I want you to count the number of British flags."

Off they went along Government Street, where every other shop, it seemed, was selling tea towels with the Queen of England's head (she is Queen of Canada too), shortbread from Scotland, pewter mugs, woolens from Britain, Burberry coats … it went on and on.

"Lots of British flags, Mom, but they're not all correct."

"How do you mean?"

"Well Mom, take this one — it's upside down."

"It is? How can you tell?"

"See the top left hand corner? Well the upper white diagonal stripe should be wider than the lower one. And if it's not, it's a distress signal. I know that from the Scouts, and I also read about it in a war story. What happened was that a British ship was captured by pirates, who then tried to sneak up on another ship.

"The British captain was under guard on deck when he saw one of the pirates hoisting a British flag, the first part of a trap to capture another British ship. But the pirate had difficulty getting it up, and allowed the British captain to help him.

"That gave the British captain the opportunity to turn the flag upside down, something nobody on the pirate ship would notice. But an officer on the British ship sure did, and knew immediately that something was wrong. When the pirate ship came close, the British ship opened its gun ports and threatened the pirates with a broadside. Well, they had to surrender — and the good guys won."

"Good yarn, Tom. Maybe you should be a writer."

They strolled back to the Empress Hotel and sat in a dining room that was like a gentlemen's club. A waiter appeared from behind a potted plant with menus.

"Fish and chips, please," said Tom.

The waiter looked shocked. "Sorry, sir, but this is the Empress — we don't do fish and chips here."

"But I thought this was a British hotel?" said Tom.

"No, sir, it is Canadian, albeit with a British influence."

"Are you British?" asked Tom.

"Actually I am, or I was."

Cathy spoke up. "What can you recommend?"

"The curry, madam."

"Is that British?" said Tom.

"No sir, it's from India. That was another of our pink bits."

When the waiter had left, Cathy explained he had been referring to a map of the world when large parts of it were British and colored pink.

"I like that," said Tom. "As of now the British are pinkos."

"I wouldn't call them that," said his mother, "that means their politics are to the left."

"It does, eh? Maybe empires are more interesting than labels. We're been reading about the Romans at school. I'll have to study the British as well."

"No doubt you will. The British empire was even bigger than the Roman Empire. Many countries used to have empires, mainly European countries. Take France, it had many colonies. In fact, for a long time Vietnam was known as Indochina and was part of the French empire."

"I'll read up on that too."

"You're going to be busy."

"No problem. I've got time on my side."

Cathy smiled and took Tom's hand. "You're just like your father — he always likes to have the last word."

CHAPTER 47
Seattle

January 1984

Christmas came and went and Seattle settled into the dark weeks of January. Not that Tom minded — the Boy Scouts had a chalet in the nearby Olympic Mountains and he was off there at every opportunity.

Like this Friday night. "Okay Mom, bye, here's the bus."

"Take care, Tom." Cathy hugged her son and helped him to the Scouts' bus with his bag and skis.

She was no sooner back in the house when the phone rang.

It was Richard Maxwell. Was she free for dinner that night, the next night, any night?

Cathy put him off politely. That night at the restaurant opening had been reported to the gossips at the office water fountain.

"Richard. You are a very nice man, and if my life was not as complicated as it is, I would be happy to have your company, but I'm afraid I can't ... I just can't. This is a small town — at least for me it is — and I have my son to think about."

"I understand that you don't want to be seen dating anyone, but can't you just come over for dinner at my place? I will smuggle you in like the Scarlet Pimpernel ..."

"Yes Richard, it could be most enjoyable, but I'm afraid I might lose my head, with or without the help of the guillotine."

It was 15 minutes before Cathy was able to put the phone down. She had to admit Richard was not lacking in charm or persistence. But her mind was made up. She was not going to compromise herself or Tom, certainly not in her hometown.

Now, when she was away ... that was another matter. Then the phone rang again.

"Cathy — it's Nick. How are you?"

"Fine, just fine, where are you?"

"In Ft. Lauderdale. I just wanted to say that in two weeks time there is a special promotional cruise, and a group of travel agents is coming from Seattle. There is a charter flight and I can get you on it as my guest. The deal is you fly down Friday morning and return Monday. The itinerary is San Juan, St Thomas and St Martin and back to San Juan. Would you like to come?"

"Nick, so kind of you to think of me. I sure would love to see you, and escape from this awful weather. Let me see what I can do. Tom has taken up skiing and he goes away most weekends. I'll see what he's up to then. Give me your number and I'll call you back."

As luck would have it Tom was planning to be at the Boy Scout chalet that weekend, and Shirley agreed to see he got on the bus and would have him to stay at her place for the Sunday night.

She phoned Nick back and said it was a go, and then got a call from a representative of the cruise line saying her air and cruise tickets were in the mail. Now that Nick was a maître d' he could make things happen.

The first person Cathy saw at Seattle airport was Ruby, the pushy travel agent from her first cruise.

"Hi hun," said Ruby, coming up to Cathy. "I remember you from that Alaska cruise. You coming with us to San Juan?"

"Hello … yes, I am."

"Good. Meet some of the others — Barb, Marg and Kath. They've never been on a cruise before but are looking forward to snaring their first sailors. That right girls?"

"Right on," said Barb.

Marg and Kath did not look so enthusiastic.

"I've never met a sailor," said Marg. "In fact I've never been on a ship before. Do you think it will be rough?"

"I'm also worried about being seasick," said Kath. "I've got patches that are supposed to prevent it. See — behind my ears."

Said Cathy, "I'm sure you will be fine. Just don't think about it. Ruby will look after you, I'm sure."

"You bet I will, girls," said Ruby, slapping Marg on the back. "The trick is to start off with a stiff drink and proceed from there…"

At that point their flight was called, and Cathy took the opportunity to make a dive for the nearby bookshop to pick up something to read on the flight.

It was a long flight to San Juan in the US Virgin Islands, but the airplane was not full and Cathy had three seats to herself. As soon as the wheels were up she spread herself across the row, put her head on a pillow, and fell into a deep sleep.

CHAPTER 48
Caribbean Ahoy!

Flight 4343 was on course, the first officer was flying the aircraft and the captain was daydreaming about the coming night in San Juan with the chief flight attendant, his girlfriend Lilya. He was soon to be on bigger aircraft with routes across the Pacific, but the downside was that his wife would want to come along for the shopping in Hong Kong, Tokyo and Bangkok. On the other hand, there would be new opportunities to meet nubile Asian flight attendants who were impressed with the authority of four gold epaulettes. Ah, and the service — when he felt like it he could put on his cap and jacket and carve the roast beef for the first class passengers.

But in the meantime he had to get this lot to San Juan. Better go and check they were not destroying his aircraft, he thought. Anyway, it was time to stretch his legs.

The captain stood up to his full six feet and two inches, sleeked back his silver hair, put on his cap and jacket, and opened the cabin door.

Just as he did so a woman in the front row suddenly stood up, turned around, and was sick over the two passengers in the row behind.

"Bitch!" yelled one of them.

"She threw up on me!" yelled the other.

The captain backed up as a flight attendant from the forward service area rushed to the passenger with a paper bag. Another flight attendant was just behind her with paper towels.

For a moment the aisle seemed clear, so the captain decided to make a run for it, but as he hurried past the second row, one of the women made to get up, putting a foot out in the process.

They locked feet in a flying embrace and the captain went down with a crash.

"Captain … my captain!" called Lilya, the flight attendant. She need not have worried. Only his pride was hurt. The captain got up, dusted down his uniform, collected his hat from a travel agent who gave him a concerned look, and proceeded on his way.

"Good afternoon, ladies," he beamed to two women midships. "I hope you're enjoying the flight."

"You've been doing a bit of low flying yourself, skipper," said the jolly woman in the aisle seat. "I hope you're all right."

"No problem, madam, although I may have broken my glasses, and in that event I may need one of you to come to the cockpit to have a look outside and help me find the airport."

"I told you we should have taken the train," said her friend in the middle seat.

"That would be of little help crossing the Caribbean Sea," said the captain. "But fear not, I have a trusty first officer and between us we will get you to, er … where did you say you were going?"

"That's it — we'll come back on the bus," said the middle seat.

The captain touched his cap and moved on, nodding benevolently to various other passengers as he made his way to the back of the cabin. Two toilets were located there, just in front of a crew service area. He chose the toilet on the right, pulled the door open — and heard the scream.

The entire aircraft heard the scream. It was emitted by Ruby, who was sitting on the toilet, her white panties around her ankles.

The captain stumbled back in shock to be grabbed by a flight attendant and then rebounded partway into the toilet, where his foot hooked around Ruby's panties and ripped them off. The captain then reeled back down the cabin with Ruby's panties firmly attached to his heel. It was not his best moment in the air.

"Captain … my captain," said Lilya, rushing from the front of the aircraft. She took his hands and pulled him back to the rear service area and sat him on a jump seat. "Don't worry, sir, it happens all the time. These stupid people who forget to lock the door."

"What do you mean stupid people," bellowed Ruby, who was emerging from the toilet. "He's made off with my panties. Look — they're around his feet!"

"You can have them back," said the captain, "with my compliments." At that Lilya picked up a pair of tongs used for serving hot meals and removed the wayward panties.

"Here," she said to Ruby, holding them up like something distasteful the dog had brought in. "They're all yours."

Two hours later the first officer landed the aircraft at San Juan, coming down with a mighty thud that made some overhead lockers spill open.

Lily switched on the public address system and announced, "As you can tell, we have landed in San Juan."

CHAPTER 49

San Juan, capital of Puerto Rico, has been receiving visitors, and others not always in a holiday spirit, since 1521. These days it's a peaceful place popular with tourists, most of whom go and marvel at the old fortress of El Morro, whose cannons once spat fire at English and Dutch pirates.

Golden Odyssey was sailing at 6 PM, so there were a few hours to spend in San Juan, just enough time for the travel agents to visit the rum factory and an opportunity for Cathy and Nick to lose themselves in the narrow streets of the old town.

They strolled hand in hand, Nick saying, "Amazing place this. We are walking on cobbles that came on sailing ships from Spain as ballast. On the return journeys the ships were loaded with gold and precious stones. You know what the ballast was then? Silver!"

"There's a shop selling silver. Let's take a look."

"Be careful," said Nick. "A friend told me he bought silver earrings at a shop in Mexico. It was a good shop too, the earrings were not cheap, and they had the hall-mark stamp of .925 — yet in a matter of weeks the silver washed off."

Shopping was out after Cathy heard that. So they went to El Morro and found the old fortress had a new purpose — as a mecca for kite flyers. Scores of brightly-colored kites flew high above the 20-foot thick walls that had been built and strengthened over the years, latterly by an Irish military engineer called O'Daly. The famous Sir Francis Drake forced his way into the port on one occasion but was repulsed, and another Englishman, the Earl of Cumberland, later managed to capture the fort, but had to withdraw after his men were laid low by dysentery.

"Shit!" said Cumberland on leaving.

Cathy and Nick strolled back through the old town and somehow found themselves on the cruise ship dock with *Golden Odyssey* just 50 yards away. They went to the terminal and found a crewman who confirmed the luggage had been put aboard and passengers only had to show ID to step up the gangway. Credit cards and other formalities would be handled on board.

Then the bus from the rum factory arrived, and when the door opened there was a scream that rippled along the dock. It sounded like the pirates were back, but it was worse. It was the travel agents returning from the rum factory and fueled up on high-octane cocktails.

Ruby was first off the bus, not with a dainty step, but pitching head first into the arms of a startled crewman who had innocently arrived to direct them to the gangway, only to find himself the recipient of the flying body of an overweight travel agent. The crewman, a young Filipino half her size, could not support Ruby's weight, and both crumpled on to the dock.

The crewman extricated himself from Ruby's flailing arms and legs and struggled to his feet, to be felled by the next travel agent getting off the bus, who completely missed her step because she was posing — in motion — for the ship's photographer who had conveniently shown up as well.

Ruby tried to get up, but her snappy cruise jacket festooned with anchors had flopped over her head limiting her vision. She tried crawling, only to get in the way of the third travel agent who had actually made it down the steps of the bus. This travel agent proceeded to fall over Ruby and as she did so grabbed for the photographer and pulled him to the ground as well.

Cathy and Nick stood stunned as the shambles unfolded. "Stop," said Nick when Cathy made to go and help Ruby get up. "This is a nightmare. Let the crew sort this out. This could get worse before it gets better."

It did. Mike Brown, the newly promoted hotel manager, feeling very smart in his uniform with four white bars, happened to be passing and came to investigate the fracas. As he got to the bus the second travel agent, she who had the ambitions to appear in a photograph, yelled, "I'm going to be ill," and she was. She delivered a stream of vomit like a projectile that covered the hotel manager's shoes up to his ankles.

"Asshole!" Mike hollered, and the travel agent screamed back, "What do you mean? Who invited you to our party? Go ..." and then she threw up again, where-upon the hotel manager turned and ran back to the ship.

"I told you," said Nick.

Jack Silver was on the deck of *Golden Odyssey* as it cleared the harbor. The sun was going down and high, scattered clouds were starting to turn crimson.

"Great night, Jack," said a passing voice.

Jack turned around and saw Robin Atkinson with a beer in his hand. "Hey, good to see you Robin, got your sticks with you?"

"Sure have. I played Dorado on Puerto Rico today, a first class Robert Trent Jones course."

"And you're here to see about a golf program for the ship?"

"Right again. Tomorrow we're in St Thomas in the U.S. Virgin Islands. And while 99 percent of the passengers are going shopping, this cowboy is heading up to Mahogany Run, one of the great golf courses of the Caribbean."

"It's that good?"

"Mahogany Run is a cracker, best known for a famous corner called the Devil's Triangle, which is actually just two holes, but that doesn't take anything away from it, because they are holes teetering on the edges of soaring cliffs with great scenery. I know guys who play there and before they hit, they stop and have a moment's silence for other men who are getting dragged around the shops."

Robin waved to a passing waiter. "Can I buy you a drink, Jack?"

"Sure, but not now. You know who's on board — Cathy Robertson. Remember her from the Med last year?"

"Sure do."

"Why don't we all meet in the bar before dinner? Also I'll see the maître d' about getting a table."

"You're on. One other thing — we don't have to dress up tonight?"

"No," said Jack, "first night at sea."

"It's just that I heard there is a group of travel agents on board and they are having a toga party."

"Oh my God, travel agents and togas. Just add booze and we're in for a right old night."

At that one of the cruise staff came by and Robin asked when the toga party was. "Tomorrow night, I'm afraid." He rolled his eyeballs. "It will be gruesome."

CHAPTER 50

Jack and Robin met up with Cathy in the bar, then they went into the dining room where Nick gave them a good table by a big window. "Not easy finding you the right table," said Nick. Then, lowering his voice, he added, "We have got two groups on this cruise — a party of travel agents, who might be a little feisty, and Bill Wilson has brought a large number of his friends. I think we want to keep them apart. And you are in the middle."

"Gee thanks Nick," said Jack. "Y'all know who Bill Wilson is? He is the founder of Alcoholics Anonymous. If you've been on a few cruises you might have noticed that every ship's daily program has an entry every day which says, *Friends of Bill W ... meet, Deck 9, starboard side ... 10 o'clock,* or similar. That is a coded message which tells any AA members on board that they have a support group they can join every day to help them stay on the wagon."

"Oh my God," said Cathy. "The AA and travel agents."

Said Jack, "It could be interesting."

"You've got that right," said Robin. "But it's not my problem. Nick, can you find the wine steward please?"

"Coming up."

Jack Silver never had to wait for his first glass of wine. While dishes arrived promptly from the galley's production line, the wine stewards, always few in number, were sometimes detained at a table for a birthday or anniversary celebration. The answer to that was to pre-order the wine, and just in case, walk into the dining room with a glass from the bar.

However, the ship's photographer was first on the scene. Dining room pictures take up much of the space in their gallery, along with the embarkation photographs. The latter are of interest to passengers on the prowl, for a picture of a young woman and an older woman, along with the obligatory ship's lifejacket, suggests it is mother and daughter traveling together — and nobody else.

As it happened May and June were on board, they who had been enthusiastically horizontal for much of that Alaska cruise. Nick met them at the dining room and showed them to a table next to the galley door. Many passengers would not have been happy with that, but May and June sat down to enjoy the passing parade of waiters.

Jack nudged Cathy. "See what the current's just blown in — the mother and daughter double act we met in Alaska. Should we introduce Robin to them?"

Cathy looked over to May and June's table. "You're right. What a small world. Robin? That's up to him." She smiled at Robin and asked, "Do you like young women, or those that are a little more mature?"

"First of all tell me what's going on here," said Robin, looking a little perplexed.

"Robin, my dear boy," said Jack, "you see these two women over by the galley door. They are a mother and daughter who hunt together. They both like young men, and I'd say you qualify, well sort of. It could be interesting."

"Tell you what, Jack," said Robin, "why don't you and I take them on?"

Cathy stood up. "I'll let you two *boulevardiers* discuss seduction tactics on your own. I'm going to bed early because I have a big day of shopping tomorrow."

CHAPTER 51

The pretty little town of Charlotte Amalie, the port for St Thomas, with its pastel, shuttered houses and narrow streets, has seen more than a little violent history and many a cutthroat, drunken sailor. That was in the good old days.

Now St Thomas is invaded daily by a fleet of cruise ships that disgorge thousands of shoppers buying everything from cameras to outsize polyester. Binoculars and electrical gadgets are labeled duty-free, but are often no cheaper than the same items sold at home, and lacking the necessary international warranties. But such is the popularity of St Thomas that normally sensible people plunge into buying expensive cameras simply because they are there and it is seen as an opportunity to save money. It's like the woman who tells her husband that she has saved him $2000 that day. How come, he asks? Well, she bought this fur coat that was reduced from $5000 to $3000.

Cathy knew all about the St Thomas trap thanks to Jack Silver. He had given her the lowdown on camera shopping: 1 — check around at home and find the model you want; 2 — have a look in St Thomas. Do not buy unless you find exactly the same model, with the correct international warranty valid in the US; 3 — the price must be substantially lower; otherwise why not support your local camera dealer? The key to it all is the warranty — in many cases St Thomas warranties are good only in the US Virgin Islands, or in Central America, or Bulgaria. If you have such a warranty and your camera has a problem in the US, you are toast.

Cathy bought a postcard and sat at a sidewalk café. She ordered a coffee and wrote to Doc.

You'd hate this place (see over) but when you come home you'll never need to visit, because I've been there-done that. Wherever you are, keep well. Tom and I think of you every day. Your loving wife — Cathy

TO THE VIETNAMESE GOVERNMENT: PLEASE DELIVER THIS CARD TO MY HUSBAND, AND THEN SEND HIM HOME. THE WAR'S OVER!

Cathy paid for her coffee and went looking for a post office.

Robin and Jack took a taxi up the busy, winding road to Mahogany Run Golf Club where they rented clubs and headed for the first tee.

"Sorry, Jack, but we don't have time to warm up as we were a bit late getting here because of the traffic."

"No worries, Robin."

"Mind you we do have time for the moment's silence to those men who are down there shopping."

Robin and Jack doffed their caps, and stood with heads bowed. Then Robin nudged Jack and said, "Let's go for it, pal."

When the game was over and they were waiting for their taxi back to the ship, Jack bought Robin a beer and mused, "You've got something here. There are lots of ships and lots of golf courses. Also lots of women who want to go cruising. The only problem is men. As women get older they get more adventurous, whereas men just get older. But if a woman can tell her lazy husband that he can have a vacation playing a different golf course nearly every day, then he's sold."

"That's why I'm here," said Robin, raising his glass. "This is good business, or will be. You don't think I do this for pleasure, do you?"

"Not at all, Robin, not at all."

They got back to the ship at the same time as May and June. They were stepping out of a taxi with two young men, one of whom Jack recognized as their waiter from the previous night.

"Hi girls," said Jack. "Had a good day?"

May straightened her pareo then pushed her sunglasses into her hair with a flourish. "We found a lovely, quiet beach, didn't we boys?" The waiter and his friend looked down as if they were looking for a deep hole to disappear into.

"The lunch was divine," said June, "But it took such a long time. I guess that's the problem with having my steak well done. Anyway, Roberto, we're got half an hour before you have to start work. Come along."

Roberto brightened up considerably at June's suggestion and they hurried up the gangway.

"Okay, Romeo," said May, "let's go for it," and she took his hand and led him up the gangway where momentarily he would, without a shadow of a doubt, thought Jack, be singing for his supper.

Jack and Robin smiled at each other with looks that said *welcome to the wonderful world of cruising.*

Cathy got back a few minutes later thinking much the same thing. Nick had been working so she spent the day on her own. She could handle the days, and on a cruise ship there was rarely a lonely night because friends were easy to make. She smiled to the security officer as he checked her ID card.

"Have a nice day, madam?" he asked politely.

"Sure did, but you were working?"

"I was madam, but doing this is not like work. I stand here and enjoy the weather, I meet a lot of nice people, and during my break I went ashore and phoned my family in Manila. Hey, life's not bad."

Lucky man, thought Cathy, and lucky family. His earnings in US dollars would go a long way in Manila, and still leave plenty to go in the bank. In a few years he would be able to go home and have the capital to start his own business. The waiters and bar staff did even better because although their basic pay was low, they got good tips. Heck, a good headwaiter could make as much as a captain, and then there was the fact that often they paid little or no income tax.

CHAPTER 52

Captain Criticos eased *Golden Odyssey* away from the dock at St Thomas and set course for the island of St Martin. It was only a few miles away. He would go slowly until they cleared the shipping lanes and then let the engines idle for most of the night.

The engines might be resting, but the captain had work to do. Some men might have relished the task that lay ahead of him that evening, but to say that Captain Criticos was apprehensive would be an understatement the size of the iceberg that sank the Titanic.

He was hosting a dinner, and as usual the guest list had been compiled by the social hostess on the instructions of the head office. Two of the names, or at any rate the combination thereof, made him shudder. One was a serious drinker, and the other a reformed alcoholic. How could they do this to me, thought the captain.

Ruby, meanwhile, was enjoyed the fruits of her promotion at the travel agency. She had been given a bigger cabin, invited to the captain's table, and was at this moment in her cabin admiring a complimentary bottle of champagne — good stuff at that. She toyed with the idea of taking it home as a gift for her husband, but as she was a little nervous, she thought she would have a drink.

Ruby peeled the foil from the top of the bottle, took off the metal fastening, and turned the cork. Or she tried to, but it would not budge. So she pushed it with her thumb on one side, then the other. POP! The cork shot out of the bottle, hit the ceiling, bounced off the side of the vanity, and hit Ruby in the eye.

Her wail reverberated down the corridors of *Golden Odyssey*. A stewardess used her pass key to rush into Ruby's cabin, where she found the travel agent holding her eye with one hand, while the other clutched the champagne which, shaken up by Ruby's cavortings, was spraying as if she had just made a Formula One podium finish.

"Madam, can I …" the stewardess spluttered to silence as a plume of champagne hit her full in the mouth. She fell backwards towards the open bathroom door and hit her head on the metal floor rim. She was quite unconscious.

Ruby tried to grab the stewardess and missed, and when she saw what happened, screamed again. This time the head housekeeper was passing. She came in and saw Ruby flourishing a champagne bottle and the stewardess laid out on the floor. It was not a pretty picture.

"What's going on here?" demanded the chief housekeeper. "Have you just murdered one of my staff?"

"Murdered? Me? I was just trying to open this damn bottle."

"What — on the girl's head?"

"Oh, my eye!" wailed Ruby, and she slumped on to the bed.

At this moment the stewardess started to come around, the ship's doctor was called, and he took her off to the clinic for a check-up, holding her arm. Before she left she explained it was all an accident, and Ruby was left to get ready for dinner.

Rodney White brushed the last speck of dust from his dinner jacket, a utilitarian number from Marks & Spencer, whose label had been overlaid with one from Armani. He checked that his bow tie was on straight, and reflected it was five years since he had had a drink. In the bad old days he would have had two gin and tonics while he got dressed, then hit the bar to start the evening's serious drinking. If only people knew how much entertaining was involved in the life of an undertaker.

It had gone downhill from there. First his marriage broke up. Then he nearly lost his business before a friend took him to a meeting of Alcoholics Anonymous. Now he was dry, a new man, and leader of his AA group's first cruise.

Rodney made his way to the card room, which had a sign outside saying *Private Party*. He pushed on the door, stepped inside, and ... saw two young women dressed in bed sheets toasting each other with large martinis. "Have a good cruise, Mabel," said the frizzy blonde loudly, "which means get pissed and laid double quick."

Her co-toaster thrust her glass into the air so that martini showered over them both and the hapless Rodney, who yelled and jumped back just as a waiter arrived with a tray of drinks.

The waiter lost his balance and crumpled to the floor, with Rodney falling beside him. The tray of drinks gathered altitude then succumbed to gravity, with four Zombie Martinis landing on Rodney's dinner jacket.

"What are you idiots doing at our party?" demanded Rodney from the floor.

The travel agents, for it was they, looked at each another.

It was the waiter who spoke. "Are you at the right party, for travel agents?"

Rodney struggled to his feet, a cherry on a stick poking out of his top pocket. "What do you mean ...?" Then he realized the waiter had a point.

"I gather this is not the function for Bill Wilson and friends?"

The waiter replied, "No sir, that's in the library."

Rodney started to back out the door.

"Stay and join us for a drink," said a travel agent.

"Er, no," said Rodney, "I think I've had my share already."

CHAPTER 53

Captain Criticos's guests were received at his cabin by the social hostess, announced formally, greeted by the captain, then shown inside where a waiter flourished a tray of wine and champagne.

Ruby and the other guests helped themselves, then set about grilling one another to establish why they were there.

Robin said he was the captain's golf instructor, there was a woman from Detroit who had racked up 100 cruises, the company lawyer and his wife were on board, and then there was the staff captain, Alex Dimitros.

Dimitros was a capable seaman but lacked a good command of the English language. However, he was handsome and smiled a lot; he could listen and the waiters came out of their blocks when he nodded in their direction. What more could a guest at a cocktail party want?

Ruby breezed up. "Hello, sailor. What's a girl to do for a good time on this boat?"

"Good evening, madam. I am pleasured to meet you."

"You might be before the evening's out."

I've got a live one here, thought Staff Captain Dimitros. "Well, this is a nice place to be, yes? See — the captain has his own private balcony. I have one as well, with a French widow."

"I heard that," said Robin, nudging the staff captain's arm. "That's what every cabin could use — a French widow, which would afford delightful prospects... It's not an original line. Delivered to the Oxford Union in the sixties I believe…"

"Sorry, I don't understand," said Dimitros.

"Don't worry about it," said Robin. "You didn't say anything bad."

"Sometimes the English language is very strange."

"The secret," said Robin confidentially, "is to get an English-speaking girlfriend and learn the language, as the French say, *on the pillow*."

A waiter topped up Ruby's champagne glass. "Any more of this and I'll be ready for the pillow, and not much else."

The captain's table was in a corner of the dining room, as far as possible from the kitchen doors, through which came a loud, crashing noise. "Hey bud," said a passenger to a passing waiter, "are you washing the dishes in there, or compacting them?" But there was no getting away from the vibration coming from the engine room down below. Just as well, thought the captain, we are going slowly tonight. Maybe I'll be able to hear what my guests are saying.

There was no missing Ruby. "Swell boat you've got here, captain," she boomed in a voice straight from the waterfront at New York.

The captain smiled benignly. "If I may say so, madam, you are not on a boat, but a ship. A boat is a small vessel that goes on a ship, like a lifeboat."

"Yeah, captain," said Rodney, for he had just joined the table after his eventful pre-dinner experience, "but is a submarine not a boat?"

"Indeed it is, sir," and with fair winds and good luck we will get to our destination on the surface and not below it."

Captain Criticos received a polite titter for his little joke, then an apparition filled his eyes. It was the travel agents coming into the dining room in their togas.

"Oh my God," said Rodney, "I thought they were not getting dressed up till after dinner."

As chance would have it they were at the next table. They saw Ruby and waved, then Rodney. "Hey," said a very inebriated woman in a figure-hugging toga, "there's our new friend. Hi there, did you find the right drinks party?"

The entire captain's table looked at Rodney. "Er, yes, I did. Nice to see you again. Have a good dinner."

"We will, honey, we will. See you at the party later. But you gotta have a toga. Right, Ruby?"

While this was going on a steward arrived with an envelope for the captain, who opened it and read quickly. "Excuse me," he told the table. "I've just received some good news and I want to share it with you. As some of you may know, the cruise line is building a new ship, which will be in service next year. I have just heard that I am to captain the vessel."

A cheer ran around the table, and Captain Criticos stood up and took a bow. He sat down and continued. "Only thing is that my presence is required in Miami immediately to deal with pressing matters. So I have to disembark tomorrow in St Martin, leaving you in the capable hands of Staff Captain Dimitros, who will have command of the ship until my return in a few days."

CHAPTER 54

Nick was enjoying his new gig as a maître d'. Everything had gone well so far, the travel agents were under control and he had remembered to tell the head wine steward to give Bill Wilson and friends a wide berth. He made his way to the captain's table.

"Good evening, captain. Is everything satisfactory?"

Captain Criticos took Nick's hand and held it up. "Ladies and gentlemen," he told the table. "This is our new maître d', Nick Pedridis. He is a rising star with this cruise line. I give you a toast — to Nick." As he was speaking a wine steward was filling up glasses around the table.

"To young Nick. May he always have calm seas, fair winds — and béarnaise sauce that does not poison the passengers!"

"To Nick!" they cried and drank deeply, as one does at sea.

Ruby slapped her glass on the table and looked around for a refill, then her glazed eyes stopped at Rodney. He looked stunned.

"I drank wine. I drank wine," Rodney repeated.

"What did you expect — mothers' milk?"

"You don't understand. I'm not supposed to drink. I've given it up."

"Well, now you're back on it — cheers! Heck, I've nothing in my glass. Waiter, a girl can die of thirst around here."

It being the captain's table, a wine steward was never far away. He sloshed a slug of wine into Ruby's glass and topped up Rodney's as well.

"Go on, enjoy yourself," said Ruby. "You look like you could use a good drink."

It was Nick who spoke next. "Ladies and gentlemen: For dessert tonight we have a Grand Marnier soufflé. It is our pastry chef's specialty and I have taken the liberty of offering this superb dish to all of you."

Being miracle workers, cruise ship chefs can make soufflés in next to no time, which was when they arrived, along with a chilled sauterne. "Ah, my favorite," said Robin to the company lawyer. "I discovered the joys of dessert wine, not in France but in Australia. It's very popular there."

"You have been to Australia?" asked the lawyer.

"Yes, I played golf there. It was part of a tour I did from the US West Coast to Hawaii, then Fiji and on to Sydney."

"Lucky man. I hear Fiji has some wonderful beaches, and good diving."

"You're right, and good curries too, as many Fijians are originally from India. It's a fascinating place, and of course it used to be quite dangerous for seafarers. The islands of Fiji were known as the Cannibal Isles, and many a shipwrecked sailor ended up in a pot.

"In fact it's not so long since there was an old chief who used to regularly take the steamer from Fiji to Sydney. His party trick was at the dinner table, where he would peruse the menu, make a disapproving face, then hand it back to the waiter saying, *Nothing interesting on this. Bring me the passenger list!*"

Nick slipped away from the captain's table and walked to the far side of the dining room. Beside a window and behind a pillar were Cathy and Jack Silver.

"Nick!" said Cathy. "Thank you for the lovely, quiet table."

"A pleasure. How was your meal?"

"Epic," said Jack. "Now tell me this — have you heard about the new ship?"

"Yes I have, but hey, I'm still finding my way around this one. And in case you haven't heard, the captain's getting off tomorrow."

"Have the travel agents beaten him up?"

"No, he has to go to Miami for a meeting about the new ship. Dimitros will take us back to San Juan."

The rest of the evening passed as predicted. Ruby made a toga from a bed sheet and joined the other travel agents. So did the Greek officers, who can smell an opportunity for a fun night at 1000 leagues. Rodney was supposed to meet up with his group for a game of Monopoly, but somehow ended up at the toga party. At 2 AM he was low-flying around the floor with a willing figure in a bed sheet. He woke up late the next morning beside the contents of the bed sheet — and blanched. As he said later, recalling the Bo Derek movie *10,* it was a case of going to bed at 2 with a 10, then waking up at 10 with a 2.

And by this time the ship was in St Martin, and all the other passengers were ashore enjoying its sandy beaches and more shopping. Robin, naturally, was playing golf at Mullet Bay. Cathy went with him.

"Can I rent clubs?" she asked when they arrived.

"You've never played before — right?"

"Right."

"Well you need just two clubs — a seven iron and a putter, and you can use mine."

They went to the first tee, where the starter greeted Robin. "Good to see you back, Mr. Atkinson. One or two playing today?"

"Just me, but Cathy here might have a coupla whacks if the going is slow."

"Aha, you've nothing to worry about there. Most of the golfers here are terminally slow. I think they watch too much golf on television. Word is that the course is building a hotel at the 10th tee."

Robin laughed. "Great idea — bed and breakfast after nine holes!"

"Away you go, Mr Atkinson, have a good one."

Robin teed up and blasted the ball 280 yards down the middle of the fairway. Then he took Cathy by the arm and explained what golf was about. Let the club do the work, he told her. Most new players, and some not so recent, think if they hit the ball as hard as they can it will go a long way. Wrong. The idea is just to swing the club, and then swing it back. Robin enjoyed teaching women because they had fewer preconceived ideas then men. Their swings tended to be more natural, more relaxed, and more successful.

They got to the 280-yard mark. Robin had 120 yards to the green.

"Right. Here's a seven iron and a ball. Swing the club a few times to get the feel of it. On your backswing take the club away low and slow."

Cathy did as she was told.

"Okay, step up to the ball. Look at it and keep your eye on the ball until after you have hit it. Remember, I said AFTER."

Cathy took the club back and up, then brought it down again. There was a satisfying smack as the ball took off, sailed through the air — and landed on the middle of the green.

"Didn't I tell you it's an easy game?"

"You did?"

And so Robin and Cathy strolled around Mullet Bay golf course, Robin playing soft, stylish strokes and knocking in astonishing putts, while showing Cathy the key elements of the game. Cathy was surprised at how enjoyable it was — not just the game, or the exercise, but the setting by the sea, with palm trees and a cool breeze off the water to moderate the heat of the sun.

"I could take to this game," said Cathy at the 18th. Robin removed his cap and kissed her on both cheeks.

"I think you should take it up. Tell you what, follow me around the world and I'll make you a tidy golfer."

"Can't do that," said Cathy. "I'm taken."

"Oh I know you are," said Robin. "and I have a feeling that you are getting closer to finding your husband. Maybe it's your unshakeable belief that you will find him — faith like that produces miracles.

"We Scots are raised on the legend of Robert the Bruce, who in the 13th century struggled for the throne of Scotland, which he believed was his right. At one time he was reduced to hiding in a cave, where he noticed a spider starting to spin a web. But the span was too much for it, and time and again the spider fell back exhausted. But it did not give up, throwing itself into the task until finally the spider made the crucial joint.

"Cathy, you remind me of the spider that tried and tried again."

"Thank you, Robin." She took his hand and led him to the 19th hole bar. Wiping away a tear, she said to no one in particular, "I think we both need a drink."

CHAPTER 55

May and June were thinking the same thing. They had signed up for a tour of the island, itself unusual in that it is shared by two countries – France and Holland. What's more, everyone gets along just fine, partly because it's a tiny little place and everyone knows everyone else, and also because they do so well from endless ships that call at St Martin.

What May and June enjoyed most were the beaches. They drove by several with brilliant white sand and palm trees.

"Romantic, isn't it, Mom?"

"I suppose so. All we need now is the romance."

Just when they thought the bus was never going to stop, the guide said, "We have a special treat for you today. We are taking a break at Orient Beach, where there is a kite-flying contest. I must warn you, however, that this beach is topless and there is also a naturist colony at one end."

"Ooh, I know what end I fancy," said May.

"Have you got the binoculars, Mom?"

"I sure have, the new ones we just bought in St Thomas. We should be able to check every dick on the beach."

When the bus pulled up the guide told them the kites were this way, the naturist colony that way, and the restaurant right opposite the bus. They would have one hour.

May and June took one look at each other, and went that way.

In five minutes they were there. There was no gate or fence, just beach where nobody wore a stitch of clothing.

"Welcome senoras," said a bronzed sunbather. "I am Roberto, and maybe this is my lucky day."

"Could be," said May, noting his muscular body and sleek, dark hair. Roberto was about 30, he was very well-endowed, and there was a ring through his foreskin. "Can I help you spread your towels on the beach right here?"

"Why not?" said May. She looked at June, whose eyes said *what are we waiting for?*

Mother and daughter then took their clothes off. All of them.

"The wonderful thing about a place like this is that you don't have to bother about remembering your swimsuit," said June.

"This is true," said Roberto. "I have not owned one for 10 years. But other men — they would not be without one. You see, if your Mussolini is small, you can stuff your swimsuit with plastic or an old pair of socks."

"Mussolini?" asked May.

"Ah yes, he was the biggest dick of them all."

"Well," said May, warming to the subject, "you don't have that problem. But tell me, what about the ring? Does it not get in the way?"

Roberto smiled and lifted Mussolini so it coiled on to the leg nearer to May. "I take the ring off first."

"I'm relieved."

May and June covered themselves with oil, particularly the sensitive bits, and laid back in the sun. A Julio Iglesias track wafted over the beach, a palm tree swayed gently in the cooling breeze, and life was good.

Then June decided it was time for a swim. She and her mother started to walk to the sea when Roberto suddenly joined them, taking both by a hand and pulling them into the water.

It was like a bath, the sand was soft, and it was heavenly. It got even better when May clamped her hand on Mussolini and found the ring had been discarded. She felt Mussolini get to his feet in about the same time it takes to say *Hail Duce!* June had the same idea but had to hand it to her mother for quick work. She knew what she had to do — set up a diversion by splashing around in the water between the couple and the shore.

Having sex under water was nothing new for either May nor Roberto, although May was at her best on dry land where she could demonstrate her astonishing ejaculations — like a washing machine emptying was how one amazed male had described the experience. What she could do right then was take a good grip of Mussolini. May had vagina muscles like a power wrench, and for good reason — she exercised her vagina muscles all day long, when she was awake in bed, or eating, reading, sitting on a bus, even while singing the Star-Spangled Banner.

Roberto beamed when he felt the effect. Mussolini stood taller than at any parade in the past, and as May worked him in her steely grip, Roberto knew that Mussolini would be on his knees before the usual number of regiments had gone by. But who cared? This was living. This was why his mother had given him extra meat at the expense of his sniveling sisters. *Mamma Mia!*

Then, where was she? What's this?

Now it was June's turn. She took Mussolini in hand and stroked him gently, coaxing him to his feet again. *Go Duce,* urged Roberto; *this is the parade of your life. Ten more regiments have to pass, and you must take the salute!*

Roberto was tired, but he felt more excited about the younger woman, and just after her mother at that. June was no slouch as well. She took Mussolini up to the top of his boots, then pressed her finger into Roberto's anus. Two regiments later it was all over.

"I like a good swim," said May, shaking the water out of her hair as she stepped on to the warm sand.

June stopped and looked round. "Wasn't this where we left our stuff?"

Roberto groaned. "I can't believe it. The Phantom has returned!"

"What are you talking about? asked May, feeling just a little concerned.

"Everything has gone — your clothes, my clothes, Mussolini's ring…"

"Fuck Mussolini's ring," roared May. "What about our bags, money, how do we get out of here without any clothes?"

Roberto put a hand on May's shoulder, and another on June's shoulder. "Look, I hate to tell you this, but our things are gone, and it is not the first time. A friend of mine, a Canadian helicopter pilot, was here last week. He had heard about the thief we call the Phantom. My friend came with no money, just sandals, shorts and a T-shirt. He took them off, backed into the water, had a quick swim all the time watching his little pile of clothes, and you know what? They disappeared! Just like that."

"Well, Roberto, pity you did not warn us," said May, "and now – see that white bus arriving at the restaurant over there? Well, we have to be on it in about 10 minutes, and we're going to be a pretty fucking picture arriving, mother and daughter, without any clothes. What do you suppose we do about it? Better still, as it was your brilliant idea to drag us into the water and leave our belongings to the mercy of the damn Phantom, what are you going to do to help?"

At that moment a breeze came up, and with it a newspaper blew across the beach. Roberto ran and grabbed the newspaper, or what was left of a day-old Financial Times.

"Here, there's only two pages. Mussolini will go without. I suggest you wrap the paper where you want and get on your bus."

May and June looked at each other. "He's right," said May, "we have no option. Okay Roberto, it's been an experience. We're outta here."

And with that mother and daughter made their way along the beach. As they crossed the line from the nude part to the prude part they wrapped the newspapers around their naughty bits. When they got to the bus the guide rose to the occasion, whistling up a couple of beach towels from other passengers.

For May and June it was not all bad — they had lost their bags but the insurance would pay for that, and they had got laid in a fairly memorable way. And the guide? He would look forward to sharing the day's proceeds with Roberto and their Phantom friend.

CHAPTER 56

Back at the ship, Staff Captain Dimitros was in charge, Captain Criticos having departed earlier for Miami. The last passengers were aboard, and it was time to say farewell to St Martin and set course for San Juan.

He picked up the bridge telephone. "Hey, Nick," he said, "you wanna come to the bridge? I know you enjoy this but also maybe you help me with my English if I make a problem."

The decks of the *Golden Odyssey* were packed with passengers as Nick made his way to the bridge. Waiters fielded trays of sail-away cocktails, and the ship's band played "When the Saints Go Marching In." It was a perfect Caribbean evening, and all was well with the world.

Until Sam, the Shanghai washerman, set the laundry on fire. He had only wanted to take a last look at St Martin as *Golden Odyssey* cleared the headland. The problem was he forgot to turn off the iron, which burned through a Minnesota's farmer's cotton nightshirt and took off from there. Sam was at the bow rail when he heard the cry,

"Smoke on the deck!" He ran back to the crew door to be met by a thick cloud of smoke. When his lungs got a whiff of it, he reeled backwards towards the rail.

On the bridge, Staff Captain Dimitros was almost directly above the crew door and he could see Sam in difficulty. He turned to a junior officer and told him to go to Sam's aid and to check on the extent of the fire.

Then he pressed the button. Instantaneously the ship reverberated with the international distress signal — seven short bells followed by a long one.

"Oh my God, what's that?" said Ruby, who was having a drink, or two, with some of the other travel agents at the deck bar.

"It's the abandon ship signal," said one of the travel agents.

"No it's not," said the barman, "it is the emergency signal. It means go to your cabins, put on your life jackets and go to your muster stations. Don't do anything else, like jump over the side, until the captain gives the order."

"C'mon, girls," said Ruby. "Let's do as he says. This could well be a night to remember."

"Whatdya mean?" said another. "That's the name of the movie about the Titanic."

A travel agent screamed. "We're all going to die."

"Don't be an idiot," said another, "we haven't paid our bar bills yet. There's no way they'll let the ship sink first."

The group tumbled down a companionway and spread out to their cabins.

Cathy was heading up on deck with her life jacket when the travel agents stormed along her corridor. "Take it easy," she said. "The ship is not sinking, you know. And it's probably not anything serious."

Up to this point Cathy had felt alarmed, but seeing the panic-stricken travel agents made her resolve to keep cool. She stepped out on to the deck and walked purposefully to Boat 3, just where the emergency drill had been held.

She was the first one there, and quickly others arrived. The casino manager was in charge of the boat, and he checked off passengers' names on a list. In a matter of minutes they were all present, including a woman with orange hair who was clutching a string of rosary beads.

The ship's pubic address system sprang to life. "This is your captain," said Dimitros, giving himself a promotion in this hour of need. "This is not a drill. This is the real thing, because fire is in the ship. I will keep you informed."

All 450 passengers stood in their life jackets on *Golden Odyssey*'s deck and waited for the next message. Would it be the dreaded *abandon ship*, with panic in the lifeboats, bodies overboard and sharks devouring women conveniently fattened up by the midnight buffets? Or would it be just a damp squib, but at least something to talk about over tomorrow's deck quoits?

They got their answer a few minutes later.

The bridge telephone rang.

"Yes?" barked Dimitros.

"The fire is out," said the leader of the fire party that had gone to the laundry. "It is just a passenger's nightshirt and a few others garments that have burned. There is a lot of smoke left, but that is all."

"Good," said Dimitros. "I'll tell the passengers the emergency is over."

He pressed the button of the pubic address system. "Ladies and gentlemen. The fire is out of control."

"*OUT OF CONTROL!*" yelled Ruby at the top of her voice.

Aaaaaaaaaaaaaah… screamed the Boat 3 passenger with the rosary beads.

Boat 5 was less retrained. All the passengers screamed.

At Boat 3, one man hollered, "Get into the boats. We'll all burn to death."

Up on the bridge, they could hear the sounds of the panicking passengers.

"Sir," said Nick urgently. "You said the wrong thing. The fire is not OUT of control. It is UNDER control."

"Here you tell them," said Dimitros, grabbing Nick's arm.

Nick pushed the button and spoke slowly, "This is the bridge. This is the bridge. The fire is UNDER control. I repeat — the fire is under control. What you just heard was an error in translation. The ship is not in danger and neither are you. You can return to your cabins and get ready for dinner."

CHAPTER 57

Human traffic jams are a fact of life on ships, particularly the big ones, and there is always a crush on the companionways — landlubbers call them stairs — after a lifeboat drill, practice or otherwise. Being an old hand by now, Cathy thought she would eliminate the aggravation by strolling instead to the deck bar.

"Cathy!" exclaimed Jack Silver, who was standing with Robin. Both wore their life jackets, both had drinks to hand.

"As luck would have it," said Jack, "our lifeboat commander happened to be the barman, so when we got the all clear we gave him a nod …"

"And," said Robin, raising his glass, "we got service that would have impressed Neptune himself."

"You guys," said Cathy, slinging her life jacket over her shoulder. "Well, I suppose it's better to toast Neptune than say hello to Davy Jones. But hey, what's a girl got to do to get a drink around here?"

A passenger at a bar is an easy mark for the cruise staff, who buy their own drinks at a special rate, but the thinking is why pay anything when the passengers are so generous? They are on vacation after all. So it was that Richard, one of the dance hosts, was passing the bar as Jack was getting Cathy a drink.

Richard was not on duty so he was able to accept a glass of wine — not the ship's plonk but a rather a more drinkable, and expensive, Chablis.

"Well Richard, what's new?" asked Jack, hoping to get something for his money.

As it happened, Richard had a story to tell. He was leaving the toga party with two women who invited him to their cabin. This was against the rules, but as there were two of them he thought it would be all right.

Cathy immediately thought of May and June. Not them again!

They were quite proper, said Richard.

Not May and June, obviously.

He agreed to have a quick drink, and sat down for just five minutes. Then he left. End of story.

That morning, he met one of the women, who returned his camera to him. Apparently he had left it in their cabin. As the film was finished he dropped it off at the photo shop — and here were the prints.

Richard handed a folder of photo prints to Jack.

"Richard, what makes you think I want to see 36 shots of you dancing with a selection of the merry widows of Palm Beach?"

"Take a look."

Jack handed a photograph to Cathy. It showed two middle-aged women wearing underwear and big smiles.

Cathy smiled and passed the photograph to Robin. "They have a good sense of humor."

"No' bad," said Robin. "I'd think ye were lucky to escape wi' yer honor, pal," said Robin.

"And my job," said Richard, taking a deep slug of his chablis. "Don't say a word, by the way."

A more savvy character than Richard would have said nothing, but he had spent his working life selling cars, and keeping quiet was not his forte. As in the motor trade, good conversation skills were extremely important for a dance host, and his partners loved Richard's fund of stories.

Now, after three years of being a perfect — well, almost — gentlemen on the high seas, Richard had met every kind of dance partner and knew what he wanted. Not so much a woman with a fine grasp of quick tempo — more one with a very large bank balance.

Such a woman was in his sights. He had known Martha almost from his first cruise, and he had established she was a widow four times over. Each husband had left her increasingly larger fortunes, she had no children, and there were no rivals in sight.

Richard cruised more often than Martha, but each time he sailed into San Francisco she would send a limousine to pick him up for delivery to her penthouse apartment on Nob Hill. Here they could have fun without staying on their feet all the time. Martha liked to say she was a clean-living girl until she moved to the neighborhood. "If you've got the name you might as well have the game," she liked to say. Mae West was her model — "it's not the men in your life that matter, it's the life in your man."

Richard had good equipment and he knew how to keep a woman happy. Not too many women, he had often bragged to male friends, had asked for their money back.

That was just an expression, of course. But now he was closing in on Martha and aimed to lure her down the aisle, putting him on Easy Street. Heck, he thought, she should know her way blindfolded by now. Martha would be on his next cruise, when he planned to pop the question.

"Richard, you're deep in thought," said Jack. "And your glass is empty."

"Oh dear, you're right, I was miles away thinking about a cruise I want to take in Asia. You know Asia, it has some dodgy airlines and airports."

"Oh aye," said Robin, "I can't wait."

"Well, panic not. When I was last there our plane made a very good landing — and quite close to the airport."

Then he was gone.

"Once a car salesman," said Jack, "always a car salesman. Everyone check their wallets."

CHAPTER 58

Dinner that night was another jolly affair as passengers worked off their relief at not having to go home in life-boats.

Cathy was in her element. Her arrival at the dining room brought her to Nick, her very good friend, who took her arm and escorted her to a prime table. It didn't get any better than this at Tara Hall. There, jumping to their feet like the true gentlemen that they were, she found Jack and Robin.

A steward stood by with a fine bottle of champagne, then a waiter presented the menu with a flourish.

"Baked Alaska tonight?" she said by way of recognizing his presence.

"Mais oui, but not to start, madam."

"She knows that, you fat frog," said Jack with a smile.

When the waiter had gone, Cathy said, "You shouldn't be rude, Jack."

"That wasn't rude. If you want to hear me doing rude I'll ask him if he has frogs' legs. If he says yes, then I'll say good order fish and chips and ask him to hop over with them toute de suite."

Later they went to the nightclub where Jack talked, Cathy and Robin danced, and groups of women waited for the Greek officers to arrive. The latter were in the crew bar. They would stay there until late, for that would give the women time to get a little drunk and maybe appreciate the altruism of the officers.

Cathy knew all about that from Nick and his friend Tony. Nick was different though — every woman's dream man. The Mr. Right of the high seas. How she adored this honest, decent man, and how much she owed to him. What lay in the future, she wondered for the umpteenth time. How long would it be before he met the right woman and married? Well, that should not be a problem; she had a husband. Or had she?

Stop it! she said to herself as her mind whirled to the music.

"You seem far away," said Robin, walking her back to the table. "What's on your mind?"

"Everything," said Cathy, squeezing Robin's arm. "Thanks for the dances. But I must go now."

The men made no effort to escort Cathy because they knew she was going to meet Nick.

They met under the stars.

"You won't believe this," said Nick, taking Cathy's hand.

"Believe what?"

"I'm going on the new ship, and I'm to be hotel manager."

Cathy kissed Nick on the cheek. "What a guy! You'll be an admiral in no time at this rate. Mind you, maybe you're keeping something from me — does your father own the cruise line?"

"Cathy — are you suggesting I would be a party to nepotism?"

"Yes."

"Well, you're wrong — unfortunately. I think I'm just lucky. The cruise business happens to be expanding like crazy at this time and some big jobs are up for grabs."

"So you'll just have to muddle through."

"That I will. I can't wait to master the intricacies of housekeeping."

"You won't have to," said Cathy, smiling, "that's why you will have a chief housekeeper. But enough of this mundane stuff. Tell me, what's the name of the ship and where will it be sailing?"

Nick took Cathy in his arms. "You know this is dangerous?"

"Yes I know this is dangerous because there are security cameras everywhere and we could end up in the next crew bar video. What has it come to that this is the extent of dangerous living?"

They both laughed, then Nick said quite seriously. "The ship is the *Ocean Pearl*, and she will be sailing in Asia. We are doing a number of cruises from Singapore to Hong Kong and vice versa. All the ports of call are in one country."

"And that is?" asked Cathy brightly.

"Vietnam."

Cathy gripped Nick's arm. "Vietnam. Why Vietnam?" she asked breathlessly.

"It's a new route. Nobody else is doing it. We'll be pioneers. Apparently the government likes our company and wants us to get the tourism ball rolling. They say most of the passengers will be Europeans such as the French, of course. Vietnam used to be the French colony of Indochina, and tourists from France will be a prime market."

"Well, I'd never have believed it," said Cathy, turning away and looking out to the moonlit sea. "One minute we are bombing the heck out of Vietnam, and now cruise ships are taking tourists there."

She looked at Nick. "Well, sign me up. Better still, it's maybe time Tom came along with me. Sign us both up.

"I'm going to take my son to Vietnam to find his father."

CHAPTER 59
Captivity

<u>May 1985</u>

Commander Robertson was alive. At this moment, however, Doc would not be saying a lot about his quality of life.

He was now medical officer at a re-education camp somewhere in far northwestern Vietnam. Make that unpaid deputy medical officer of health.

He lay down after a 10-hour work shift and cast his mind back 13 years to that last flight. Doc's aircraft was hit by a missile near the port city of Haiphong. He ejected safely, then came down near a coastal gun battery. At least, he reflected as his flying boots crunched into sand, he would not be getting his feet wet.

Doc barely had time to unfasten his parachute harness when a squad of soldiers arrived and took up position around him, rifles trained at his head. Then the soldier in command stepped forward and indicated to Doc to raise his hands.

This he did, and the lead soldier searched Doc, taking his handgun and knife, as well as his wallet and watch. Then another soldier stepped forward with a piece of rope. Doc's arms were grabbed and his hands tied tightly behind his back. The rope cut into his wrists and he cried out in pain.

The lead soldier barked a command and the knots were slackened. Doc smiled, bowed his head and quietly said *cam o'n ong/ba* — thank you. He thought back wryly to his buying the Vietnamese guidebook so he could talk to patients he might encounter in a postwar situation. Now the shoe was on the other foot.

A truck arrived and the lead soldier indicated to Doc he was to get in the back. Doc climbed in with difficulty and took a seat towards the cab with soldiers all around, guns still pointed at his head. They were all young, and one of them had trembling hands. Doc noted with concern that one finger was twitching on the trigger of his AK-47. Hope it's not a hair trigger, thought Doc. He looked away from the soldier in case it made him more nervous.

The truck got under way and was soon in a town busy with traffic, albeit mostly bikes and cyclos — the rickshaw of Vietnam that is a three-wheel bike with a seat for two in front of the rider. Doc was just starting to take in his surroundings when the lead soldier came to sit across from him and said *zin loi* — sorry — and held up a piece of cloth. He was to be blindfolded.

Nothing Doc could do but bend his head forward and submit. Oh well, he thought, it could be worse.

It would be. Hours went by and although Doc could tell he was on a main road, it was in poor condition with potholes that shook the truck and jolted Doc's back against the uncompromising wood seat and a vertical metal support that stuck in his back.

Finally the truck stopped, a rifle poked him in the ribs, and Doc shuffled to the end of the seat, then a hand grabbed his flying suit and yanked him down. Doc tumbled on to the ground, landing heavily on his shoulder.

An angry voice was yelling at him in Vietnamese and he guessed this was a request to get up. This he did with some difficulty, then several pairs of hands grabbed his arms and pushed him along. He heard doors opening and closing, then a different kind of door — a metal one — and a hand ripped off his blindfold and pushed him forward. Doc fell headfirst on to the concrete floor of the cell.

CHAPTER 60

Welcome to the Hanoi Hilton.

He was kept in isolation for a week, then interrogation followed. Doc was asked the name of his ship, how many aircraft, what targets, how long the ship would remain in that location, where it would go next, what about morale, and more. In every case he answered with his name, rank and serial number.

Doc steeled himself for the beatings that inevitably followed. Doc had seen much human suffering, which he thought, would prepare him for the physical assaults inflicted on his body, but it still hurt. He thought back to what he had read about torture, that 99 percent of the time it was brutally effective. The human body and mind can take only so much. Doc prepared himself for the time when he would submit, consoling himself with the thought that he had little information of use to the enemy.

The worst of it was the food. What there was of it came once a day on a metal plate. It was always the same — stale rice crawling with maggots. Without hesitation he closed his eyes and ate it. Everything. And he chewed the maggots, convincing himself they were simply small snails — escargots was the word he reached for. The garlic sauce was missing, so Doc had to imagine that.

He could certainly picture what would happen if he did not eat what was on his plate. There was a precedent he knew about — of a friend's father who was captured by the Japanese when Singapore fell in the Second World War. He was thrown in Changi Prison and fed a similar diet for more than four years. The food was revolting and many men refused to eat it; some tried but could not force it down. Years of good living, including many a dinner at Raffles Hotel, made it hard for men grown soft. So they died.

One morning, perhaps a week after his arrival at the Hanoi Hilton, Doc was taken, not to the interrogation room, but to face a senior officer.

"Sit down," said the officer, dismissing the guard with a curt wave of his hand. "My name is Tang. Tell me about yourself. I understand you are a medical doctor as well as a flyer. Tell me about your work."

Doc had no problem talking about that.

Tang heard him out and said, "There is work for you here, helping the children of Vietnam. Many have been injured, in body and mind, by the American bombing, and we have been forced to set up special hospitals in remote areas to treat them. You are going to such a camp."

Doc said he appreciated that, but surely there was work for him here in Hanoi, and he would like to stay with his fellow prisoners, some of whom undoubtedly needed medical help.

Tang barked, "That is not an option. Your colleagues are war criminals — you are a war criminal. You are lucky to be alive considering how the American criminals are bombing, killing and maiming the Vietnamese people. The government in Hanoi is being generous in giving you the opportunity to repay the Vietnamese people for their suffering. You will leave tomorrow."

On the day of his departure Doc was allowed into the exercise yard for the first and last time. He was alone, but he could see faces — American faces — behind bars in the windows. He looked in every window, nodding and smiling, as he went by. The faces looked back — blankly, other than one. Doc did not recognize the shrunken eyes amid the stubble of a beard, but they seemed to know him. Doc slowed his pace and made to mouth "good to see you" but as he did so a rifle-butt slammed into his back.

Doc stumbled, but managed to carry on. Then he was back in his cell.

CHAPTER 61

Lieutenant John Parker was the man in the cell who recognized Doc. He had wanted to call out his name but knew it would have resulted in a beating for the man in the yard. Parker was also from the Kitty Hawk. He had been shot down a year earlier, suffering a badly broken leg in his parachute landing. He would be one of the first prisoners released when the war ended, and in his debriefing Parker reported seeing Doc alive in the Hanoi Hilton.

The following morning the door of Doc's cell was thrown open and two guards grabbed him, tied his arms behind his back, and pushed him down a corridor. Moments later he was in the back of what seemed to be an armored truck; certainly it was solid and he could not see out. In fact he sat in the dark, alone as far as he could tell, but with his bound hands now lashed to the frame of his seat. The engine started with a deep, diesel rumble, commands were shouted, and he was off.

Doc had no idea where he was going, but the truck driver knew the road well. The route exited Hanoi and headed to a camp in the jungle, a place unknown to the military of South Vietnam and the Americans. Even in North Vietnam it was a closely guarded secret.

Doc wondered what he would be required to do, what conditions would be like. Would there be a hospital with trained staff and essential equipment? Doc wondered about many things, not least about Cathy. By now she would know he was missing. Would the North Vietnamese report that he was alive?

Sometimes the North Vietnamese authorities did report that an American was being held, or that he was dead, but more often they did not. Why assist the enemy? And in the case of Doc, there was no way anyone was going to know his fate, for he was going to a place that was most secret.

When Doc finally emerged from the truck it was dark. He had no idea how many hours he had spent on the road or what time it was, but there was enough moonlight to see he was behind a high fence with guard towers — and the outlines of huts.

Doc was led to a small hut. A guard shone a flashlight on a bed, pushed Doc inside, and closed the door. Doc heard a bolt being drawn. He lay down and slept the sleep of an exhausted man.

The next day Doc was taken before the camp commander.

"I am Cam," he said. "You have been told that this is a camp for children. I have to amend this information, which contains an economy of the truth."

He continued, "This is in fact a re-education camp for dissident people in Vietnam — Buddhists, reactionaries, those who do not share the vision of our esteemed leader Ho Chi Minh. Some are young, but in fact children are in the minority, and we would rather they all stayed alive while we show them the error of their ways. That is your job. We have doctors, of course, but they are engaged in looking after Vietnamese people who are supporting our struggle."

And so Doc was put to work. There were more than 600 people in the camp; he was the only doctor and the only American. There was a small medical clinic with limited facilities, but it was clean. He did not have many medicines but there was disinfectant, and through vigilance and good luck the camp avoided any epidemics.

CHAPTER 62

Soon after Doc's arrival Tang got a report from the camp commander that Doc was a model prisoner, working as well as he could with the children and the adult patients. Tang had told Doc that it was a children's camp because the re-education camps were highly secret, and he did not want Doc to know any more than was necessary until Doc was safely inside the camp. Of course he could have said nothing, but Tang was a wily intelligence man who believed that a little disinformation was better than none at all. Keep them guessing — preferably confused — was his style.

Also, if they were useful, keep them happy. And that was where Kim came in.

Kim, which means gold, was a Vietnamese nurse assigned to assist Doc. She was not an informer, not a spy, rather a nurse who had been asked to work in the camp and had gone without question. Tang had no doubt that nature would take its course.

Doc was smitten the moment he saw Kim. He was captivated by her dark beauty, eyes like pearls and long hair tumbling down the back of her ao dai, the elegant trouser suit that is the national dress of Vietnam. Her hands and feet were delicate, her body slender and surprisingly tall for a Vietnamese. And she had a shy smile that lit up her face like a frangipani in the morning dew.

She spoke no English, but soon began to pick up words, then phrases, and her teacher was Doc. When their work was done she and Doc had their evening meal together, and her company saw Doc through the days.

Doc and Kim were moved to a small hut that was part of the administration block of the camp. He had a room with a cot and a desk and chair. Kim, who was nearby, had just a cot. Their toilet was a latrine dug near the perimeter fence and their shower was a bucket with holes in the bottom. Exercise was a walk around the fence, always in view of armed guards in watchtowers.

Before they became lovers Doc explained to Kim that he had a wife in America. He paced the floor of his tiny room and said quietly, "I am a prisoner. One day I hope to leave this place, and if I do go with my mind intact, it will be thanks to your company. My feelings towards you are strong," and Doc held her hand and looked into her deep, dark eyes, "and I am a man and very weak, and I am finding it harder to resist your charm, but when I leave I will be alone, and I want to say this to you now."

Kim took his hand, pulled herself up, and kissed Doc gently on the mouth. Doc put his arms around her, then ran his hands down her *ao dai*, feeling her nakedness underneath. Doc lowered her on to his bed. And so Doc and

Kim began an affair that would comfort them both in the many, long days that followed.

After dark was the worst time. Doc would lie in his cot listening to the sounds of the night, the cicadas and frogs, while the nearby jungle provided a cacophony of roars and grunts, and sometimes the wind and rain howled through the trees. Aircraft flew overhead constantly, big ones flying high, and he guessed they were American B-52 bombers. He wondered if the Kitty Hawk was still at its station off the coast, or had it gone home?

Home. Did Cathy know that he was alive? That face in the window at the Hanoi Hilton — had this man been freed, but had he recognized Doc? He did not know.

All Doc did know was that he was alive and that he was being surprisingly well-treated at this camp. And then there was Kim, just a girl of 18, his only friend in this alien land.

CHAPTER 63
Hope and Despair

When the US involvement in the war ended on March 29, 1973, nobody told Doc. But he eventually found out when the camp began to receive an influx of detainees. This time they were mostly officials from the South Vietnamese government in Saigon, as well as some senior officers from the defeated army. Doc's hopes soared with the possibility of an early release.

But it was not to be. The camp continued to operate. There was more work for Doc, and Cam, the camp commander, refused to see him. It was clear there were no plans to repatriate Doc.

The reason was as simple as it was cruel. The victorious government in Hanoi had decided to retain what it saw as a key group of prisoners to be used as bargaining chips with the Americans. It was Doc's bad luck to be one of them.

CHAPTER 64
Vietnam

September 1985

But Doc was not forgotten, not by Cathy, nor by the Navy, and finally not by Tang, the intelligence officer Doc had met at the Hanoi Hilton.

Many changes had occurred in Vietnam since the end of the war. Although communism was still the order of the day, the Vietnamese are as naturally entrepreneurial as the Chinese, and the economy had began to function again. The railway service from Hanoi to Saigon, now renamed Ho Chi Minh City, also got a new name — the Reunification Express, and a few tourists trickled in. They were backpackers mostly, but they brought with them hard currencies, which the government badly needed.

In return the tourists got Dongs to spend. One traveler was a female business reporter from Hong Kong, who wrote favorably of the budding economy, but she could not resist wondering if anyone could take the currency seriously until it got a new name.

Tang, now in charge of trade and tourism in the Hanoi government, argued that the best way to boost the economy was to make peace with its neighbors, and America. No progress could be made, however, until the American government was convinced that all service personnel, dead and alive, were returned. He asked for a list to be compiled.

Then he reached into the tray on his desk and found a message that a cruise line was soon to make a series of calls at Vietnamese ports. The ship was arriving from Singapore and proceeding to Hong Kong, and the company had permission to stop at Ho Chi Minh City, Da Nang, Halong Bay and Haiphong. From Haiphong the cruise line proposed to fly passengers to Hanoi for a day visit.

Tang put down the file and lit a cigarette. Then he pushed back his chair and thought about it, but not for long, because it seemed to him this was the kind of tourism the new Vietnam needed — a limited number of people, presumably wealthy, who could easily be monitored. It would be a simple matter to show them what suited the government of Vietnam, and the tourists would go home with the impression that this was a responsible regime struggling to recover from the maladies of aggression.

One week later a file marked Prisoners landed on Tang's desk. It was in two parts — Dead and Alive, with the first part fairly lengthy and the second part just one page. Tang scribbled an order to prepare the bodies of the dead prisoners for repatriation, then scrutinized the list of captives. The only name he recognized was Robertson, the Navy flyer he had met at the Hanoi Hilton. He asked for a report on the location and circumstances of these men.

Then he thought about Robertson. As Tang recalled he was in a re-education camp working with reactionaries and Buddhists. Some children too, if he remembered. It had been a long time and by all accounts Robertson had acquitted himself well. Of course there was the girl too. Tang smiled and commended himself on his prisoner involvement experiment. In the Second World War the Japanese had brutally mistreated their captives, which resulted in low work rates and humiliation for Japan at the end of the war. Tang had studied this and opted to try for the carrot rather than the stick. Kim was the carrot — a delectable carrot by all accounts.

Now the war was over and Vietnam wanted to make a great leap forward, as their Chinese cousins had done. It had to use cunning.

Tang came up with a plan.

CHAPTER 65

Doc was getting dressed in his usual cotton shirt, pants and sandals when Cam, the camp commander, walked in.

"Commander Robertson, I have good news for you."

"Any news would be good news, Cam. You know I have been trying to see you for years. The war is over. Why are you holding me?"

"I regret that relations between my country and yours have not been normalized. But now things are changing. My instructions are to send you to Hanoi. You leave in one hour. Please be ready."

And with that Cam turned and left.

Doc went directly to the clinic where Kim was taking the blood pressure of a Buddhist monk. He waited till she finished and with a turn of his head urged her outside.

"Kim," said Doc urgently, "this is it. I have just been told I am leaving here. I am going to Hanoi and I don't know if I will be returning."

"So this is what you call goodbye?"

"I think so." Doc took Kim's hand and led her behind a screen. "This is a moment I have waited for, because this is not my home. But I have dreaded it too, because you and I have been close."

Doc looked tenderly into her eyes, afraid he would see tears. But Kim was smiling. "Go, my brave friend. You have done well here, and you leave me with memories I will treasure. Go, to your country, your friends, your wife. Go with my love." And she reached to his lips with hers and kissed him as lightly as a raindrop.

When Doc opened his eyes Kim was gone.

Doc turned and went back to his room. On the bed was his flying suit and boots. Cam was there as well.

"Take these with you but do not wear them until you are so ordered. There is a truck waiting. Good luck." Cam reached out and shook Doc's hand.

Eight hours later Doc was in Hanoi, where the truck stopped at a hotel. Tang was waiting outside.

"Welcome, commander," said Tang. "We have a room for you here, and we must talk."

Doc looked up at the hotel's name — the Hanoi Sunrise. "Glad to see it's not the Hilton."

Tang led him inside, followed by two guards, and they went to a room on the second floor, where the guards positioned themselves outside.

There was a tray of tea, and drinks as well, including beer. "Help yourself," said Tang. "Here's a menu, choose what you would like to eat. I'm afraid it's all Vietnamese food, but you will be used to that."

"What's going on?" asked Doc.

"You're going home," said Tang.

"When?"

"You'll find out soon enough."

Doc reached for a bottle, found the opener, and took the top off. "I think I need a drink."

"You deserve it," said Tang. "I am sorry you have been kept here so long. It was not my decision. But we have arranged a little send-off, I think you call it, for you."

Doc sipped the beer. "Yeah — a firing squad at the airport?"

"Not quite. But there will be a parade of sorts, and a medal."

"A medal — for what?"

"You gave great assistance to many Vietnamese people. You came as a war criminal and you leave as a man who has paid his debt to society."

Tang bowed, shook Doc's hand and left.

CHAPTER 66
Meanwhile...

Cathy and Tom landed at Singapore's Changi Airport at dawn. The arrival formalities were thorough, for Singapore is nothing if not security conscious and very efficient at it. But the officials were friendly as well, and smartly turned out, all of this in no small part due to Singapore's British heritage.

"I like this airport, Mom," said Tom with the enthusiasm of a 12-year-old boy. "It's so clean. Hey, what about that sign — Chewing Gum Prohibited."

"They mean it as well. One wad of gum in your mouth and it's big trouble. Like an on-the-spot fine that will take care of your pocket money until you are in college."

"How come? Since when was chewing gum a federal offense?"

"Think about it, Tom. Think about the gobs of gum that stick to carpets in government buildings, on the sidewalks — hey about that time just recently when my friend Sheila got some on her jeans. Some prat had left chewing gum on a seat. Hey, even when it gets on your shoes it's not a lot of fun. So here they decided to do something about the menace — like ban it. That's Singapore — they don't just hang around and worry about problems — they act on them. Drugs are another thing. They have the death penalty here for drug dealers."

"Wow," said Tom. "I'm on my best behavior till we're outta here."

The bags came up quickly, then it was on to customs.

"Anything to declare?" asked a customs officer asked, politely.

"Not a thing," said Cathy.

"What about jewelry?"

"I don't travel with jewels, other than a few costume items. Oh — I have a small piece of gold." Cathy fished in her handbag and produced the airplane charm Doc had given her."

The customs man examined it more out of his interest in airplanes. "Fourteen carat," he said, "nice airplane, but pity about the gold. In Europe women prefer 18 carat, but here it's 22 carat. That's real gold."

"I've heard that. But in America we don't buy gold to put under our beds. Fourteen carat is fine for jewelry, and anyway, this has great value to me. It was a gift from my husband."

"Well then," said the customs man. "It will be safe here in Singapore. Have a good visit."

He waved them through with a smile, and there was a young man in a blazer holding a sign for *Ocean Pearl*.

"Welcome to Singapore, I'm Peter Black from the cruise line. We have a bus waiting for you outside if you'll just follow me."

There were a dozen other passengers on the bus, whose driver was a cheerful Chinese man who said he was Ong. "That is my name but all my friends call me Off," and Ong roared with laughter.

"Well, kid," said Cathy, "now you know American bus drivers looking for tips don't have a monopoly on good one-liners."

The bus stopped at the Raffles Hotel, and when they got out Cathy held Tom back. "Let the others go first. I want to take my time here. This is a special place."

Tom knew the story already, of how the Raffles was one of the great hotels of the East, along with the Oriental in Bangkok and the Peninsula in Hong Kong, hotels widely known when travel was relatively rare. They were more like clubs used by an exclusive band of traders, bankers and a moneyed elite. Smart hoteliers like the Sarkies brothers, who were Armenian, catered to this demanding clientele. There were others, of course, like the Norfolk in Nairobi, the Mount Nelson in Cape Town and Meikles in what had been the British colony of Rhodesia. Legendary stories were told about them.

Kenya's Lord Delamere, for example, liked to start an evening at the Norfolk with a brace or two of Tusker beer, and ending up by drawing his revolver and shooting bottles off the bar.

The Long Bar at Raffles saw many a riotous night as expats from rubber plantations partied with sea captains, while in more recent times the Tiger Bar was the hangout for military types, one of whom presented a poster that hung behind the bar. It showed a Royal New Zealand Air Force jet firing a missile, and the caption (borrowed from a US phone company's advertising slogan) said *Reach out and Touch Someone…*

Cathy and Tom had a room facing the garden, one that smelled a bit fusty and had a fan that stirred the air with little enthusiasm. But it was spacious and had comfortable furniture. Tom flopped into a big chair and wondered out loud who had sat there before him.

"Pity it can't talk," said Cathy. "Have you seen a safe?"

Tom scurried around the room, looked in wardrobes and under the bed. He shook his head.

"Right," said Cathy. "I'll leave our passports and tickets with reception, where there will be a safe. And our little piece of gold may as well go there too."

"Mom, that's the charm Dad gave to you?"

"Yes. I believe it's a Navy airplane, one your father flew."

Tom took the charm. He held it up to the light, his fingers under the wings, and made an arc with his arm. "Mom, can I wear this? You know, like round my neck. It will be safe there."

Cathy sat on the side of the chair and put her arm around Tom. "Of course you can. Let's get going and we'll find a shop to buy a chain. Mind you, it won't be 22 carat."

At that the phone rang. It was Nick.

"Well, what does it feel like to have your own hotel on water?"

"It would be better if all the cabins' plumbing had been connected up properly. It's not the fault of the workers here — they just didn't have enough time. Anyway we've had to hire extra technicians and there are just finishing the job. But enough of that boring stuff. How was your journey?"

"Long, but no problem. Staying in Raffles is an experience, and now we are looking forward to seeing your new ship."

"New she is not, but she's got character, and the right ship for our adventure. Look, I have to go — see you on board."

CHAPTER 67
Vietnam by Sea

Captain Criticos stepped on to the bridge of *Ocean Pearl* and grinned to himself. This was not every captain's dream. On the long flight to Singapore he had been reading about the big, sleek transatlantic racer called the *Queen Elizabeth 2*, or QE2 as she was better known. *Ocean Pearl* was quite unknown — just an old Baltic ferry.

But, thought Captain Criticos as he stroked a piece of gleaming brass, she was well built — strong enough indeed to handle Baltic ice — nimble like a ballet dancer to get into small ports, and her shallow draught would be perfect for the Saigon River. As a ship this was not a promotion for him, but he would not want to be anywhere else. With this little ship he would be setting off on an adventure that was the stuff of boys' magazines.

Vietnam no less! What was more, the South China Sea and other waters around these parts were stiff with pirates, modern-day Barbary Coast robbers who rode speedboats to prey on freighters and ferries. So far no cruise ships had been attacked, but there was always a

first time. With that in mind Captain Criticos checked a
tall cabinet behind the navigation table, unlocked it, and
was pleased to see inside two rifles, two shotguns and six
handguns. The ammunition was in another locked cabinet
in his cabin.

The phone rang and he picked it up. "Captain here."

"Front desk, sir. All passengers on board."

"Very good. Ask the hotel manager to call me."

The phone rang again.

"Hotel manager here sir."

"We are about to leave Singapore. As we clear the harbor we enter the roads, where passengers can see hundreds of vessels of all sizes riding at anchor. It's an
amazing sight. I would like to give a commentary but I'll
be busy, even with a pilot at my side. Can you do the job
please?"

"Aye aye, sir," said Nick. "And by the way sir, good to
have you in charge."

"Thank you — and congratulations on your appoint-
ment."

Minutes later *Ocean Pearl* slipped her moorings and
pointed her bows into the setting sun. Even without
Nick's exhortations, few passengers would have missed
being on deck. It was not just the number of vessels at
anchor, but the constant traffic all around: pilot boats
scurrying to their charges, ferries nipping under *Ocean
Pearl*'s stern, deeply-laid lighters towed by straining tug-
boats taking ships' cargoes to the docks. It had been like
this since soon after 1818 when Stamford Raffles landed
here under the noses of the Dutch, who considered the

Malay peninsula their domain. Raffles raised the British flag and declared Singapore a free trade port.

Tom Robertson nudged his mother. "You know Mom, I would like to have been here with Raffles. I mean, at my age I could have been a midshipman on a Royal Navy frigate, and eligible for a share of the spoils of victory."

"Or," said his mother, "thinly sliced by pirates' cutlasses."

Tom ignored that, turning his attention to a junk anchored just off the channel. "Look at that — a real Chinese junk. No sails mind you — it's probably diesel-powered."

"Don't you believe it," said a voice from behind. "It's got 20 pairs of oars and when the slaves are being well whipped it can take the captain waterskiing."

"Jack!"

Cathy flung her arms around the broad shoulders of Jack Silver, who gave her a long squeeze, then turned his attention to Tom. "Is this who I think it is?"

Adult affection doesn't always go down well with kids, but Tom was enchanted. He had never seen his mother so spontaneously happy and he had looked forward to meeting this man.

Tom held out his hand.

Jack took his hand, and beamed. "So you're the guy. I've heard a lot about you. And now we get the opportunity to get to know each other. We're going to Vietnam, which should be quite an adventure."

"Just what I was saying," said Nick, joining the group.

"Hey Nick, good to see you," said Jack. Then, stepping back, he stroked the four white epaulettes on Nick's shoulder and added, "Well done. You must be the youngest hotel manager on the seven seas."

"Well, the job isn't too glamorous at the moment. We have problems in some of the cabins. It's these new vacuum toilets. Yours working okay?"

Everyone chorused positively.

"Mine's great," said Jack. "And boy, is it powerful. You know what Tom — if you and I could organize all the passengers to flush their toilets at the same time, we could be across the Gulf of Thailand in an hour."

The voyage across the Gulf of Thailand to the South China Sea was as the captain planned — sedate. It was cruising as good as it gets. The water was calm and the tropical sun was moderated by a cool breeze. Singapore is just 200 miles from the Equator, and can be unbearably hot — a sticky situation gladly left behind by *Ocean Pearl*'s thrusting propellers.

Sea days are marvelous for getting over jetlag, and the long flight from Seattle to Singapore, via Tokyo, came with lots of that. Cathy spent two days under an umbrella on deck sleeping most of the time, while Tom roamed *Ocean Pearl* from the bottom of the engine room to the bridge.

Yet it was over the side that intrigued him most, like the flying fish, which really did take to the air as they skimmed from wave top to wave top. And then there were the dolphins — what performers they were. Tom got permission to go right to the bows of *Ocean Pearl*, where, with a rope tied round his waist as ordered by the captain, he had a spectacular view of school after school of dolphins ducking and diving as they kept pace with the vessel.

At other times Tom stood at the ship's rail and looked out over the South China Sea. This was where his father's aircraft carrier had been based. His father had been here, had flown these skies, and with luck, was somewhere over the horizon. Tom put his hands together, closed his eyes, and prayed,

Dad, this is to let you know we have never forgotten you, not for one minute, and now we are coming to see you, to bring you home, so I hope you are praying too, and that you hear this message from Mom and your son. My name's Tom, I'm 12 and Mom says I look just like you, although I'm not as tall of course. Keep well Dad — I love you. Tom.

CHAPTER 68

Dawn was breaking as *Ocean Pearl* arrived at the muddy brown waters of the Mekong Delta and prepared to navigate the Saigon River. A pilot boat appeared out of nowhere and moments later nosed alongside *Ocean Pearl*, idling at two or three knots. A door in the side of the ship opened, and helping hands reached out to pull the two pilots on board. It would have been easier if the pilots had not been carrying briefcases, but pilots the world over always carry briefcases. The whisky and cigarettes have to go somewhere.

Captain Criticos welcomed the pilots to the bridge and let them get on with it. The pilot in charge, a short, fat little man with bad teeth, went to the helmsman, pointed out the river entrance, and said "Allez."

The helmsman did not know French but got the gist of it. Just to be sure he turned to the captain, who nodded his assent. Captain Criticos leaned back in his high chair, lit a cigarette, and marveled at the changing times. Just 30 years ago this part of the world was Indochina and officially part of France.

The Saigon River is not wide so *Ocean Pearl* picked her way carefully all morning. Nor was the landscape of long grass particularly alluring, but the traffic made up for that. At first it was men in canoes fishing with nets, then more canoes with men and women in conical straw hats, standing up and rowing in a distinctive manner. The movement appeared to be in reverse, but it was graceful and more like a dance step than a rowing motion.

Then buildings began to appear, and when they got bigger the passengers crowded to the port side for the first sight of downtown Saigon — or Ho Chi Minh City, as it was now known.

Ocean Pearl tied up beside a dismal dock that was brightened up by welcome banners and a group of children, who sang and waved flags.

"What are they singing, Mom?" asked Tom.

Cathy shrugged.

Jack Silver put his arms around them both. "Tell you what — it ain't the Star-Spangled Banner."

He lifted his binoculars and said, "Hey, see all those porcelain elephants on the dock? These are BUFEs — every GI brought one back to the States."

He got two blank looks in return.

"You don't know what a BUFE is? Well, I have to tell you, but it ain't pretty. Tom, you'll have to excuse my language."

"Oh, I'm sure he's heard it," said Cathy.

"A BUFE is a Big Ugly effing Elephant. You'd be amazed at the number of American basements that have them, not to mention garage sales. But hey, if you want to buy one it won't cost more than five bucks, and they're not bad. Just the thing to go beside the fireplace."

An hour later Cathy and Tom were in a cyclo, at that time the best way to see Ho Chi Minh City, whose narrow streets were a churning mass of 50,000 of them, as well as bicycles and not too many cars. In a cyclo the passengers have a slowly-moving ringside seat of an absorbing Asian city.

Their driver spoke not a word of English, but when Cathy asked for the market in French he understood immediately.

"Hey Mom, are we going shopping?"

"Yes and no — you can't beat a market for getting an idea of the daily life of a people. And if you must know, I want to buy black pepper."

One dollar took care of the driver and they stepped into the market. It was huge and crammed with hundreds of stalls. But it was not crowded, and Cathy and Tom felt quite safe as they strolled around, fascinated, at the sights and smells. Cathy found the black pepper quickly, and bought a kilo for $1.

As they turned away from the pepper stall, a man confronted them.

"Good afternoon, you are from the ship?"

Cathy looked at him. He looked Vietnamese, wore the typical baggy clothing, and had a handsome, open face.

"Yes, we are. Who are you?"

"I am Duc, a student of English. Will you permit me to say a few words of English to welcome you? It is also good practice for me."

"Sure — perhaps you can help us. We could have taken a shore excursion organized by the ship but we would rather explore by ourselves and meet people — well, like yourself."

"Thank you. There are two things you must see — the Cu Chi tunnels and the War Crimes Museum."

"I've heard of the tunnels, that's where the Viet Cong used to hide, but I don't think that's my cup of tea," said Cathy. "I don't like confined spaces. But what's this museum?"

Ten minutes and a cyclo ride later they were at an ordinary-looking building on a small, dusty street. Duc led them into an anteroom with a desk. One dollar covered the admission for all three of them.

The museum appeared to be a picture gallery, and they were pictures of death: young and old, men, women and children, victims of the war with the Americans. They had been shot, burned, run over by tanks, some dead, others as good as. They had missing limbs, hair burned off, faces gripped with fear and shock. There was no doubt who was being blamed.

Cathy took Tom by the hand and whispered, "Let me say this, war is a brutal business, and we know that the Americans did not always fight fairly, but one thing I notice right away is the one-sidedness of all this. To look around here you'd think the Americans were the only bad guys, but I don't see any pictures of Viet Cong atrocities."

Tom was taken aback by what he saw, but could still manage a perceptive comment. "Well Mom, I hope I'm not just making excuses for our guys, but I look at the suffering here and ... well, our sailors at Pearl Harbor probably didn't look any different."

They came to a door at the back and stepped outside, and Tom couldn't believe his eyes. It was a military graveyard, a US military graveyard with enough equipment to fight a small war. At his feet was a machine gun, next was a field gun, over there a helicopter, and one thing Tom could not miss — a Navy aircraft, a battered Douglas Skyraider. No Crusaders, he was relieved to see.

Tom stepped gingerly around the weapons. What became of the men who had used them, he wondered. Had they died in a swamp, in a jungle ambush, or had they been caught in the open like Custer at the Little Big Horn? Or was this simply obsolete equipment discarded in a dump and now dragged to this eerie place? His father would know.

"Tom — come and see this."

He went to the very back of the yard and saw it — a guillotine.

"You know what that is?" said Cathy. "That's from the time the French were here. When they wanted to execute people they didn't use a rope or a firing squad. They brought this baby from La Belle France and applied basic French justice — off with the head, just like the revolutionaries guillotined Louis XVI and Marie Antoinette."

When it was time to leave, Cathy asked Duc to take them down Dong Khoi, which in the days of the French was called Rue Catinat. It's a narrow street running down to the river, and not particularly impressive, but it had a memorable moment soon after the defeat of the French forces at Dien Bien Phu in 1954.

A long column of the Foreign Legion marched down Rue Catinat to their ship, backs straight, heads held high, singing La Marseillaise. Vietnam had triumphed in yet another of the many wars that had befallen the country. The Americans would be next.

Duc accepted $1 from Cathy. "I leave you now. Thank you for your time, and for the lessons in your language, which I hope I spoke okay. Can I also say that despite what you have seen today there is no longer any problem between Vietnam and America. The young people growing up know little of the war, and those that do know it, want to forget, to build new lives. We want to make money, to have McDonald's."

"McDonald's!" exclaimed Tom. "My favorite."

"My brother is in Hong Kong and in his opinion McDonald's is better than communism. One day I will follow him and use this money to buy a Big Mac."

Cathy and Tom laughed, shook Duc's hand, and went on a cyclo back to *Ocean Pearl*. They did not want to ask how his brother had got to Hong Kong, or how Duc proposed to go. They had heard of Vietnamese refugees escaping the regime on fishing boats, rafts even, and falling into the hands of pirates.

CHAPTER 69

"Evening madam, welcome back to the ship," said Ocean Pearl's security officer.

Welcome back to another world, thought Cathy. Mind you, she reflected with a wry smile, the one on shore was not all bad. The people were friendly, the sights and sounds were pure gold for the curious traveler, and with a fistful of $1 notes you could just about buy the place.

Back in their cabin, Cathy found the ship's program and what caught her eye right away was Cocktail of the Day — and the special was Tony's Treat.

Could it be the same Tony?

Cathy and Tom later went by the bar to take a look. It certainly was, and he was not alone.

"Cathy!" exclaimed Diane.

"Well, fancy seeing you here," said Cathy, extending a hand. "Or maybe I shouldn't be surprised."

"The main reason I came along, other than my passion for Vietnamese food, is ..."

"...your passion for ..." cut in Tony.

"… don't say it!" Diane laughed wantonly, then stopped abruptly. "And who is this young man?"

"Ah," said Cathy. "This is my son Tom. Tom — this is Diane, whom I have met on previous cruises, and this fine fellow behind the bar is Tony, star bartender of Ocean Cruise Lines."

Tom shook hands with Diane and Tony. "Coke for you, young man?" asked Tony.

"And what about Cathy? Would you like to try my treat?"

"Er, no thanks," said Cathy quickly. "I want to stay on my feet for the next two hours at least. What about a glass of dry, white wine? Have you a chablis?"

"I do, but it's expensive. What about this chardonnay from Chile? We just got it on board and it's a nice little number."

"Sold."

The drinks were just arriving when Richard the dance host rolled up.

"Richard, your timing is perfect, as always," said Tony.

"Hi all," said Richard. "I won't have a drink at the moment, though. I'm waiting for Martha."

"Wonders will never cease," said Jack Silver, arriving at the bar. "Well I'll have one, Tony. Make it a Low Flyer, with a dash of water."

And so another convivial shipboard evening got underway, although the ship did not. *Ocean Pearl* would remain docked overnight with all passengers and crew on board. The Vietnamese government had relaxed restrictions on visiting foreigners but had been less generous with cruise passengers. If you arrived by land or air you were free to go out at night, but docks were military areas, and as such off limits after dark.

It was no great loss, however. The passengers had been ashore all day and were happy to be back on board where it was cool, there were hot showers and staff who recognized them and would do their bidding. Like serving dinner. The large group of French passengers sat at designated tables and talked excitedly about their adventures. Few spoke English so there was little communication with other passengers, other than two couples from the French-speaking part of Canada. The latter were bilingual, and they felt just a little superior to the other French whose lack of language skills condemned them to traveling in a group. The French, on the other hand, looked down on the French-Canadians as country cousins. One who had lived in England was heard to say, within earshot of the French-Canadians naturally, that the latters' accent was so bad she would prefer it if they spoke English.

CHAPTER 70

Cathy, Tom, Jack and Diane got to the dining room to-gether. The maître d' smiled and said, "Ah, the guests for the hotel manager's table."

Jack nudged Cathy. "Nothing like friends in high places."

Moments after they sat down Nick hurried in. "Sorry I'm late."

"Not the toilets again, Nick?"

Nick laughed. No, they are all fixed, but not before one exploded."

"Exploded!" said Tom.

"Well, not like you are thinking, but let's say it back-fired in an unfortunate way while a French woman was … but I think I should spare you the details."

The wine steward timed his arrival perfectly…

And Cathy looked at him closely. I know that man, she thought.

"Marco!"

"Yes, ma'am, we met on a cruise to Alaska, I believe."

"You're right. Well, lovely to see you again."

"The pleasure's all mine, ma'am." Then, nodding to Nick, he continued, "The hotel manager has chosen some excellent wines for tonight, and as we are in Vietnam, which used to be French, the wines have a French accent. So, we start with a white Burgundy, a Macon Villages, and for the red drinkers we have an Aloxe-Corton."

A waiter arrived with the first course and Cathy unfolded her napkin, then she sensed something. She was putting the napkin on her lap when it clicked — her dress was revealing, too revealing. Cathy had a silk scarf over her shoulder, which she rearranged around her neck with a view to avoiding further distractions. It was not what she wanted on this cruise, certainly not with Tom at her side.

Jack, meanwhile, was entertaining Diane with quotes by passengers, such as "Do the crew sleep on board?" and "How do we know which photos are ours?" Or his favorite — "Should I put my luggage outside the cabin before or after I go to sleep?"

"People can't be so stupid," said Diane.

"You bet," said Nick. "I was once in a little tour boat in Greece, and one man asked the captain if the sea went all the way around the island."

The table erupted with laughter, which encouraged Nick to carry on. "That was just half of it. The captain started his emergency drill saying, … 'In the unlikely event of this vessel sinking again…!'"

Nick's table shook with laughter once more. Now Jack weighed in. "What about the time I was in the Greek islands, and this dope said, 'The Greeks sure built a lot of great ruins.'"

Tom nudged his mother. "Tell me, is this what happens to adults when they go on a cruise?"

Jack put his hand on Tom's shoulder. "Young man, it gets a lot worse than this, I'm afraid. Just wait until we've finished the wine."

"Someone looking for me?" And Marco was back. He flashed a glance at Cathy and was disappointed that the swelling bosom he had noticed earlier was now well-covered. Oh well, he thought, this was not a table where he should be sticking his neck out.

But the net result of the dinner was that Cathy went to bed very much aware that she was still an attractive woman. Good, she thought. She would not like her husband to find her otherwise. And what would it be like if and when she ever found Doc? The sex, that is. Would he want her after all these years? Would he be able? She had heard of prisoners being ill-treated and suffering terrible injuries. Doc might look at her blankly, or worse still become violent. Cathy pulled the sheet around her neck and rolled over. Enough of this nonsense. Sleep!

CHAPTER 71

Ocean Pearl spent two days cruising the South China Sea. It was not as the cruise line would have wanted, but the Vietnamese government would only allow four stops on the itinerary. The weather was good, however, and the passengers spread themselves around the decks and cooled off in the pool. Tom was intrigued to see that the pool was drained and covered every night, then refilled with fresh seawater. Trapshooting was scheduled for one afternoon, and Jack Silver was delighted to hear that one passenger had actually asked if it would be held outside.

Jack and Tom got on very well. Tom was amazed that anyone could get paid for being a travel writer. It had to be the best job in the world, certainly after flying a Navy fighter airplane.

Da Nang is not the prettiest place in the world, but during the war it was a huge supply base for American forces; at one point transport airplanes were coming in at such a rate it was the busiest airport in the world.

Ocean Pearl came alongside the dock soon after first light. But even at this early hour there was a welcome band and children waving flags. Jack Silver was on deck and he strained his eyes to see what kind of flag. Whatever it was, it was not the stars and stripes. The band struck up and he was surprised to hear "When the Saints go Marching In." That was the safe option, thought Jack, recalling the time a North Vietnamese government minister on a visit to an African state stepped off his plane and was serenaded by a band playing the national anthem of South Vietnam. The bandleader was last seen heading for the nearest border.

A gangway was run up to the ship, and local officials came aboard to clear the ship. They had, of course, large briefcases.

Half an hour later the officials returned to the dock, staggering down the gangway with their booty. As they disappeared into the customs house the captain announced that the passengers could go ashore.

Everyone had signed up for the visit to Hoi An. It certainly seemed that way to Cathy and Tom when they made their way to the gangway deck, which was solid with people, some of them packing the companionway they were trying to go down.

"Whoops," said Cathy, pulling Tom back. She whispered to him: "This is something you get on cruise ships with older people, groups, or simply passengers who have not travelled much. They love to line up. They are afraid of being left behind, they want to be first ashore to get the front seat on the tour bus — I don't know why, but they are a pain."

After a short time the line began to move, and then the pace picked up so that they got to the smiling Vietnamese immigration man almost at a trot. The reason was not hard to see. The immigration man was only glancing at their identity cards, which was fair enough as his colleagues had just been on board to check the ship's papers and passenger and crew passports. And get their whisky and cigarettes of course.

As they got to a bus they met Jack Silver, who nudged Cathy, "You know, every time I go through an identity check at some distant place I'm reminded of the character in a boys' magazine in Britain. He was a sort of secret agent, always getting into tricky situations at border posts. Invariably he would save the day by producing an official-looking passport-type document in a weird foreign language, which he would pass off as a visa, or letters of transit as featured in the move *Casablanca*. The funny thing was that the document was the rules of cricket in Portuguese!"

They were on the last bus, and almost at the back. Cathy nodded to passengers she recognized as they squeezed down the aisle that was built with smaller people in mind. Same went for the seats: fine for two slender Asian people but under severe strain when sat on by substantial American backsides. One row had four fairly bulky passengers, which meant slabs of flesh were hanging over the aisle on either side as Cathy, Tom and Jack came by.

"Breathe in everyone!" said Jack, who was bringing up the rear, so to speak.

The back seat had room to spare for the threesome. "Well," said Jack, whispering in Tom's ear, "now you know what to do if one day your pants won't fit. Give up the burgers and fries and try a bowl of rice instead."

There was a grinding of gears and the bus lurched off. However, it was a short run to Hoi An, where the convoy disgorged a motley collection of Western tourists in various shades of beige, tennis shoes and hats ranging from Chicago golf caps to remnants of the Foreign Legion. The good people of Hoi An took little notice, however. It was not so long since the area had been overrun with American servicemen, and for hundreds of years before that the little port had attracted many vessels from other trading nations, mainly China and Japan.

Many Chinese put down roots, building shophouses on the waterfront. This type of building has a store on the ground floor and the merchant's home above. It is common in China, of course, and in other parts of Asia, such as Penang, and particularly Singapore, where these buildings have been destroyed in the name of progress. Hoi An's claim to fame are three streets of well-preserved, 18th Century, wooden-fronted shophouses, some of whose owners have not been slow to embrace tourism.

Cathy, Tom and Jack went to the establishment of Koo Ji Won, where seven generations had made good livings from trading tea, rice and silk and goodness knows what else. Poem-boards hung from the walls, which in turn were permeated with aromas of teas and cinnamon. Jack loved such places. To him this was the fabled East, the very place Christopher Columbus had been trying to reach when he set off from Spain in 1492.

Mr. Koo bowed to the esteemed visitors. Naturally most of them bought something. Cathy, for one, spotted fresh vanilla and the price — four times what locals paid — was still a bargain compared to what she would pay at home, assuming she could find it.

The Chinese were not the only settlers, for one of the main attractions in Hoi An is the Japanese Covered Bridge — a small, red structure that has been rebuilt several times in the same, simple 16th Century design. Inside it has statues of two dogs and two monkeys, suggesting that work on it began in the year of the monkey and ended in the year of the dog, or vice versa.

"Right," said Jack, "we have time to go to the museum, or the market. I suggest the latter."

"Lead on, MacDuff," said Cathy.

Jack laughed and said, "You've been associating with that Scottish reprobate Robin Atkinson!"

"Well, I wouldn't put it that way. He is a friend, and I enjoy his Scottish way of saying things."

"That's true. He is a character."

"But I don't suppose we'll be seeing him on this trip. Not many golf courses in Vietnam."

"True," said Jack.

The market was on the river, and it immediately reminded Jack of the floating market in Bangkok. As in the Thai capital, farm produce and fish were brought to the market in long, narrow boats. But whereas the Thai boats had engines — usually car motors slung on a pole and thus called long-tailed boats — the Vietnamese vessels had oars, and were rowed by women who stood facing forward, pushing the oars in that elegant motion that was like a dance-step. They wore long, loose-fitting gowns and conical hats, they smiled easily, and thought Jack, were the prettiest picture this side of San Francisco.

Most came ashore and sat on the ground, their goods displayed in front of them. Local women were there in force, with fish appearing to be the best seller. But there was more.

"Oh my God," said Cathy.

"What's the matter, Mom?"

"Don't look Tom."

"You mean the dogs? Hey, nice puppies." Then he turned to his mother. "Mom — I know these are not for pets. I saw a TV program once about how they eat dogs in China. Here too, I guess."

"Well, I'd rather not think about it," said Cathy, turning away and looking a little pale.

At that point some French passengers came by, followed by Diane and Tony. "Hi guys," said Diane breezily. Then she noticed the puppies. "Aren't they cute? Tony — shall we take one back to the ship?"

"No way, Diane — ships used to have cats on board to catch rats, but never a dog. Anyway these puppies are …"

Before she could finish Diane had started talking to a Frenchwoman who was also interested in the puppies. Trouble was, the Frenchwoman spoke no English, and Diane's French was, well, limited.

"You got dog?" said Diane to the French woman. "You know, dogez-vous?"

Tony took Diane's arm. "Time to get back to the bus." He looked at Jack and Cathy and gave a look that said, boy, what I have to put up with to get laid.

CHAPTER 72

Ocean Pearl sailed that evening, and in the darkness passed close to Hue, the once-magnificent imperial capital that took a battering in the American war. Cathy lay in her bed and read about Hue, wondering how can these people possibly forgive us?

Back in Hoi An, Mr. Koo counted a wad of US dollars before putting them under his mattress. It was, he thought, good to have the Americans back.

The next day the South China Sea was serenely calm for *Ocean Pearl*. Nick allowed himself a break from his office and met Cathy on deck.

"Well," he said, "isn't this the place to be? Look at the sea, what an amazing color of green it is, like the waters off Hydra in Greece. There is no wind, and the sky is a soft blue like your eyes…"

He stopped with a smile as Cathy poked him in the ribs. It was her way of reminding Nick he was more brother than lover.

"Some friend you are, Nick," said Cathy in mock disdain. "I've hardly seen you since we got on board."

"Ah, with the big job comes big responsibility," said Nick. "Which reminds me, I have good news and bad news for you. Which would you like first?"

"The bad."

"Okay, our visit to Ha Long Bay is in doubt because the agent forgot to tell us that we are there on a public holiday and the tour boats are not working."

Cathy knew about Halong Bay, where a French director would make the movie *Indochine*, a visually exotic movie that revealed to the world the mystical scenery of the bay, an astonishing array of 1600 limestone rocks rising out of calm waters edged with a honeycomb of caves.

"Is the trip off then?"

"No, I've suggested using the ship's lifeboats. I remember once in Venice a British troop carrier anchored in the lagoon when the gondoliers were on strike. The Royal Navy was not going to let the gondoliers spoil their fun. The captain simply lowered a ramp and out came half a dozen amphibious vehicles, which proceeded to drive straight up the Grand Canal. The gondoliers were furious, but the British soldiers and sailors did not miss out on anything. And it was free!"

"Can we do that?"

"The captain is checking."

"And the good news?"

"Everything is confirmed for Hanoi. There will be two chartered aircraft and they will do as many round trips as necessary. It's only a short flight from Haiphong to Hanoi. I'll see you and Tom are on the first aircraft."

At that moment Nick's radio called him to the bridge. "Got to go. It's probably about Halong Bay. I'll see you later."

Cathy watched Nick leave, then turned and looked out to sea. Flying fish were skimming the waves, easily keeping up with the ship pushed by its pounding engines. They could only be doing this for fun, thought Cathy, not like salmon which take to the air only when they are being chased by whales, or trying to get up a river with hostile waterfalls. But what she was seeing out there was not a struggle to the death, and that gave Cathy's heart a lift. Soon she would be flying, and to Hanoi, where Doc was last seen. What awaited them, she wondered anxiously.

CHAPTER 73

At the aft end of the ship, on the Lido deck, lunch was being served. Martha had invited Richard to join her, which was the only way a dance host was allowed to sit down with, let alone have lunch with a passenger.

"Richard darling," said Martha confidentially, "once again it is sheer magic to be on a cruise with you. Do you think we could be as happy together on shore?"

Before Richard could reply, Marco the wine steward arrived. "Madam, I have the Chablis you ordered. This is the best vintage we have. Will this be all right?"

"Let Richard try it. He's more of a connoisseur."

Marco poured a little wine into Richard's glass. He took a sip and beamed. "Perfect. Definitely not corked." What he did not say was, "Whew, this is the real thing, not the rubbish I'm used to drinking at home."

"Cheers, Richard darling. So nice to be with a cultured man who knows his wines."

The Royal Navy could not have done it better at Halong Bay. *Ocean Pearl* anchored off the entrance, lowered its boats into the South China Sea, which co-operated with perfect conditions, and off they went.

Once again Jack went with Cathy and Tom. The lifeboat's diesel engine chugged steadily as they absorbed the dramatic scenery, made even more interesting by a slight mist over the sea. Jack said it could be caused by the heat or by air pollution, because there was a big industrial area not far away.

"Gee," said Tom, "you mean you've got factories in a place like this?"

Jack put his hand on Tom's shoulder. "Listen buddy, not so long ago I was on a hotel barge cruise on the River Seine in France. We started at Giverney where the painter Monet had his studio, went through Paris, and into Burgundy. And what do you think we saw on the other side of Paris? Cement factories! One round every other bend in the river."

The lifeboats circled the craggy rocks for a while then headed for shore to visit the grottos. Tom and the others scrambled ashore at the Hang Thien Cung cave, and strolled, wide-eyed into a huge chamber glistening with sparkling stalactites and stalagmites. Because the tour boats were tied up for the holiday, they had this natural wonder all to themselves. Or did they?

While they were in the cave a speedboat pulled up at the dock and four men got out. Jack, who had separated from the others, saw them arrive and thought it might be trouble in the shape of officials who did not approve of their using the ship's own boats.

As they got closer Jack saw three of the men were indeed wearing uniforms. Senior Army officers, by the look of them. But the third was not. Hang on a minute, he thought, I know that man.

"Robin!"

Stone the crows, thought Robin Atkinson, not Jack Silver!

The two men hurried forward and threw their arms around each other.

"What are you...?" both asked at the same time.

"Well," said Robin, " I should not be surprised to see a well-traveled man like you here, so I should explain. These gentlemen are with the Vietnamese Army, which is planning to build a hotel on the waterfront near here. This is a popular tourist place, as you can imagine, and while up to now it has been mostly tourists from Vietnam and China, they want to get Japanese tourists. And Japanese tourists are crazy about golf, so that's where I come in."

Just then Cathy and Tom joined them, which led to more joyous greetings. Just to cap it all Nick stepped ashore as well, and without hesitation he invited Robin to come aboard for dinner. The Vietnamese Army officers, who up to that point had felt a little bewildered if not left out by the exuberant reunion, were visibly cheered up when Nick invited them back to the ship as well.

CHAPTER 74

The ship's bars were buzzing before dinner. It had been a good day ashore and everyone was looking forward to Hanoi the next day.

Richard had just finished his stint on the dance floor, taking great care to step out with all the ladies in the room. Too many dances with the same passenger would be noticed — not by his boss the cruise director, but by the other women. He had the last dance with a heavily perfumed giant of a woman from Texas (the dance hosts called her the Tank) then followed Martha to the bar at a discreet distance.

The only seats were at the bar, where Diane was perched, as usual, keeping a close eye on Tony. They joined her, and she in turn introduced a Frenchman called Jerome.

"Ah, Napoleon's brother!" said Richard.

"Oui," said the Frenchman, who was happy to show off his English. "You know France then?"

"Mais oui, I go there a lot on cruise ships. I like stopping at Nice, and Monaco as well."

"Ah, but Monaco is not part of France."

"True, but French people certainly enjoy it, even if they can't keep their money there, not like the Germans and Italians."

"That's not a problem. We keep our money in Switzerland. But the Italians! You know," said Jerome, warming up to the subject, "because they are afraid of kidnapping in Italy, the rich people there drive modest cars. But then they come to Monaco. They drive in a Fiat and park it safely underground. In the next stall is a Ferrari, which they drive to the bank to collect their jewels. Up in their apartment they have their Brioni suits and Hermes shoes. The women have their mink coats and couturier clothes. For a few days they make a big splash in Monaco — dinner at the Hotel de Paris, gamble at the salon privé in the casino, maybe take a trip in their yacht. Then they put the furs away, take the jewels back to the bank, park the Ferrari, and go home in the Fiat. It's crazy."

"Good story," said Richard. "I like the Ferrari bit. I've always wanted to drive one."

"I just got one. I'm getting married and my fiancée give it to me as a wedding present."

"Martha — did you hear that? Remember we were talking about living together rather than being married? I think you would look wonderful in a wedding gown."

Tony chipped in, "Oh go on Martha, don't be a spoilsport. You're only middle-aged once."

"You men!" said Diane in mock horror. "Money and sex — that's all they think about."

"Oh I don't know," said Richard. "I think I'd like another drink."

Nick hosted a table for Cathy, Tom, Jack, Robin and the three Vietnamese Army officers. Only one of the soldiers spoke English, and marginally at that, but there was much toasting (probably learned from the Russians, thought Jack), rapid inebriation, and smiles.

Tom asked what was the best thing to see in Hanoi. There was silence for the reply, "You must see Uncle Ho's mausoleum. *Velly solly* — we call him Uncle Ho, you call him Ho Chi Minh. Then you cross road to Army Museum and see the MiG jet. It *velly* special."

"That all?" said Tom.

"Much more. But this most important."

"There you are, Tom," said Robin. "You have your instructions. Doesn't sound too hard."

Jack coughed. "Well, we have a set itinerary and no deviations are allowed, but my understanding is that the Army Museum and the mausoleum are on the tour."

Jack stood and toasted friendship between America and Vietnam. The Vietnamese officers drank without emotion.

Same when Nick got up and toasted goodwill between Vietnam and all nations.

Robin said, "A man's a man for all that," and all three got to their feet and chorused, "To the workers' hero, Robert Burns!"

"I tell you," said Robin with a satisfied smile, "Robert Burns sure gets around."

The next morning *Ocean Pearl* docked in Haiphong. The weather was perfect — a clear blue sky, no wind, 65 degrees. Robin would have said it was just right for golf. As it was Robin was back on shore, pacing out golf holes for prospective Japanese tourists.

Cathy and Tom were in the first bus to the airport, which drove through the outskirts of the city. A guide on board apologized for the poor state of some of the buildings. "It is from the war. We had much bombing."

Tom looked at his mother and fidgeted uncomfortably with the airplane charm he wore around his neck. I hope the guide doesn't recognize this, he thought.

At the airport they boarded a twin-jet aircraft without delay. Tom saw it was an elderly Tupolev, a converted Russian bomber. But the inside was clean and smart, and there was plenty of legroom. Emergency signs were in English, including one for an escape rope, saying, "Throw out and climb down." He wondered if it was 30,000 feet long. Then they were in Hanoi.

And so was Doc.

CHAPTER 75

That same day in Hanoi Doc awoke in the Sunrise Hotel, had a shower and put on his flying suit. It felt good to have it back, and he noted happily that it still fit him perfectly. His flying boots had been nicely shined, but when Doc put them on they felt stiff and heavy. Well, for more than 10 years he had worn nothing more on his feet than sandals.

There was a knock on his door. It was Tang.

"Good morning, commander. How are you today?"

"It depends. What have you got planned for me?"

Tang sat down on a wicker chair and indicated to Doc to do the same.

"First of all I want to say that I am most sorry that you have been detained after the war. Can I also say that there was much anger at what the Americans did and many of the cadres wanted to keep all Americans prisoners and work them to death."

Doc was tempted to interrupt, but he bit his tongue. Tang offered him a cigarette, which he refused, then Tang continued. "As I told you before, times have changed, and you will be freed today. It will be a formal ceremony with a declaration by the Vietnamese government that all American servicemen, alive and dead, are being returned home forthwith."

"I see," said Doc. "Sounds interesting. Do I get to go home alive, or do I get publicly shot and sent home in a box?"

Tang laughed. "You Americans never lose your sense of humor. No, I will personally see to it that you are de-livered, very much alive, into safe hands. There should also be a reporter there as well, for we are now allowing western correspondents in Vietnam."

"Good," said Doc. "I will remember to smile for the cameras."

Cathy gripped Tom's hand as they walked from the aircraft at Hanoi airport. Clutching their passports, they entered a grubby building with a bad smell and peeling, dark green paint. Men in uniforms sat at elevated desks so they could look down on arriving passengers. The *Ocean Pearl* passengers waited their turn, then reached up to present their passports.

"You from ship?" a man in a field grey uniform asked brusquely. But he was smiling. And he got down from his high chair and walked round to meet the Americans. Holding out his hand, he said to Tom, "You are very wel-come in my country. I know you have just one day here. I hope your short visit is productive and you understand that the Vietnamese people are your friends."

"Thank you," said Tom after a moment, somewhat taken aback by the unexpected enthusiasm of their welcome.

As they left the immigration building and walked to their tour bus, Cathy put her arm around Tom. "Well, to think that only a few years ago we were dropping bombs on this place."

The bus filled up quickly thanks to the friendly and efficient reception by the Vietnamese authorities. A guide got on board, and the bus was then waved away by an official in what looked like an Army uniform.

Then the bus was trundling along bumpy roads in the company of trucks belching black diesel fumes, as well as some Army vehicles, some sporting mounted weapons. There were few cars, other than the occasional official-looking limousine. But, like Ho Chi Minh City, there were hundreds — make that thousands — of bicycles and cyclos.

Tom, at 12, was not overly interested in girls, but he had to admit that they looked very pretty in their flowing trouser dresses. The *ao dai* is always enchanting to visitors of Vietnam, although not all realize the significance of the colors. Girls wear white for purity, older unmarried women have soft, pastel colors, and matrons wear strong colors. They all have conical hats, a necessary guard against the sun, but worn with the right piece of gaily-colored silk, it can be a fetching fashion item as well.

The bus came in from the west and turned into Hanoi's Old Quarter just before the Long Bien Bridge. Tom had done his homework and knew that this Red River crossing had been a target of huge importance in the

American war. Had his father bombed it? He felt his heartbeat pick up.

Traffic was heavy now, and the bus crawled through groups of cyclists, stopping several times when cyclo drivers cut in front. Another time a small motorcycle with four on board — including two small children — came scarily close.

Cathy scanned every face, looking for one that was white. Or would Doc not be burned by the sun after all these years? Would he have been working in a hospital, or out in fields? She did not know. She clutched her handbag, which had copies of letters she had written to the Vietnamese government saying she was coming. Surely, if he was alive, this was the time to let him go. For the love of God, the war was over. Then she remembered the ruling Communist Party had banned all religions, including Buddhism. Okay, what did atheists believe in? Did they understand mercy? She began to feel anxious. Unconsciously, she reached over and took Tom's hand.

The bus pulled up near a small lake, and the guide announced they had a short walk to the Museum of Independence. In fact it is was the home of Ho Chi Minh when he wrote the declaration of independence for Vietnam in 1945. The group filed through, respectfully checking the contents of the display cases and the pictures on the walls. But it was a dry place that meant little to Tom. He tugged on her arm and they went outside to get more of the atmosphere of the city. Throngs of people went by. They all wore the same kind of clothes, long loose-fitting shirts and baggy pants, which looked comfortable and cool. Few took any notice of the Westerners standing outside the house. For all they knew the *Ocean Pearl* group were Russian contractors. Maybe the baseball caps some wore were a giveaway, but it was none of their business. That's what happens when authoritarian regimes are in charge.

After what seemed like an age, the rest of the group came out of the Museum of Independence and followed the guide to a market. For once Cathy was not in a mood to shop for black pepper. Instead she stood outside and again watched the people in the street. Tom did the same.

Cathy put her arm around Tom. "This is crazy. Here we are in Hanoi, standing on a street corner and expecting your father to walk by."

"He might."

"Yes, he might." Cathy felt a tear start to run down her cheek. It took her by surprise. She had not felt particularly like crying. Her eyes were not even red. In fact this was as emotional as she had felt in a long time.

"Mom, Dad's been here. I know the Hanoi Hilton is not far away, maybe two or three streets south. They won't let us go there, but this is close."

Cathy took a handkerchief and wiped her eyes. As she did so Tom took it from her gently, and did the same. They turned and put their arms around each other, and cried tears of frustration.

They hardly noticed the group leaving the market, but one of the guides saw them and directed them to follow the others, who were walking along a wide avenue, which turned out to be Dien Bien Phu, named after the decisive jungle victory that ended the French war.

Tom and his mother tagged along after the group, stopping momentarily to drink from the bottles of water they had brought from the ship. They both noticed an open area on their left where troops were arriving in trucks, then, on their right, they found the Army Museum, a white, arcaded building left over from French colonial days.

But the building was nothing compared to what was in front — a MiG 21 jet fighter on a plinth that was made from what looked like scrap metal.

They went closer. The scrap metal had markings from US military aircraft. There was no doubt about it — the plinth was clad with wreckage from American aircraft shot down over Vietnam. Cathy and Tom stood breathless. It was a brilliantly powerful, evocative piece of sculpture. No doubt about who won this war.

Tom swallowed hard and moved closer. Several aircraft markings were visible. Were any Navy Crusaders? He could not tell. Tom stepped backwards and took in the whole picture.

Cathy tapped him on the shoulder. "I'm going inside. Follow me when you're ready."

"Okay mom, I'll catch up with you."

And so she left Tom transfixed, wondering where in the pantheon of war sculpture the experts would put this epic.

Then he heard the soldiers cheering.

CHAPTER 76

Tom turned around and looked across the road to a square. The soldiers were lined up on three sides, and a platform party was arriving. He could see flags — one he did not recognize, presumably the Vietnamese flag, but the other looked familiar.

Tom walked to the side of the street. Traffic was heavy on both sides, but he chose his moment and dashed for the middle, and then did the same to get to the other side.

Both the flags were in full view now. And one was the Stars and Stripes. The soldiers were cheering, so it was some sort of celebration. But what could it be?

Then a man spoke, "Hey kid, you lost?"

Tom turned and met the reporter from the *South China Morning Post* in Hong Kong, an American called Dan Onslow.

"Hi," said Tom nervously, "I'm with my mom, or I was. We're on a tour across the road. I came over to take a look."

"Join the party," said Dan, who was wearing a camera around his neck and carrying a notebook. "This is a special occasion. Apparently they are releasing an American pilot, and giving him a medal as well. Seems he is a doctor who did some good work at a remote prisoner-of-war camp for many years. The Hanoi government wants to show they have a change of heart and want to be friends with us…"

"That's my dad," blurted out Tom.

"Your what?"

"It must be my dad. He's a Navy pilot. He was shot down 13 years ago. I've never met him," said Tom, starting to smile. "But I will now."

Dan's mouth fell open. Heck, he thought, this is some scoop. "Kid, what's your name …"

But Tom was on the move towards the platform, where a tall, handsome man in a flying suit was shaking hands with an official in uniform.

"Dad!" he called out, and started to run.

Doc looked up to see a fair-skinned, tousle-haired boy, in jeans and checked shirt, running across the open square. Hundreds of armed soldiers were on three sides, but none made a move to stop him.

"Dad! It's Tom!"

The boy jumped on to the platform and stood before his father.

Doc's eye caught the airplane charm, then the young boy's face that pleaded for recognition. And he understood.

Doc stepped forward and took the boy in his arms, and as he did so a huge roar of cheering when up from the soldiers.

Tom spoke as his face pressed into the flying suit, "Dad, your wife is Cathy, right?"

"Right son," said Doc. "Cathy Robertson. I'm Commander Jim Robertson, and I'm coming home."

He turned to Tang, who was smiling widely. "I don't know if you had a hand in this, but thanks anyway."

"Let's just say we knew your family was going to be in Hanoi."

Doc turned back to Tom. "Your mom's here?"

"Yes Doc, I'm here," and there she was. Cathy had followed Tom across the road. Now he embraced his wife, and then all three hugged together. The soldiers cheered for all they were worth, for it was now clear what was going on.

"I guess my last visit home was kinda productive," said Doc to Cathy. She ran her fingers through Tom's hair. "You could say that. Another pilot in the making, I'd say."

Tang cut in, "You are free to go. I've made arrangements for a car to take all of you to the airport, where you will join the flight to Haiphong, and then leave on the cruise ship *Ocean Pearl*."

"Sounds good to me," said Doc. "Anything else?"

"Yes," said Tang with a smile. "Here's your medal. We didn't get around to giving it you today. You gave much help to the Vietnamese people."

"Don't mention it," said Doc. He took Cathy's hand, and Tom's hand, and they all smiled for Dan Onslow's camera.

POSTSCRIPT

THE POW ISSUE

This was hugely emotive for many Americans, and significant numbers, including many celebrities, wore bracelets with the names of POWs. Following the end of US involvement in the war in 1973, and the release of 591 American POWs, activist groups maintained there were more US servicemen being held in Vietnam and Laos, and urged the US government to investigate reports of secret POW camps.

In 1985, a Sylvester Stallone movie about POWs who had been left behind, was released. Called *Rambo: First Blood Part II*, it was a big box office success.

THE MEN

COLE BLACK, who grew up on a farm near Lake City, Minnesota, spent seven years in the Hanoi Hilton where he was brutally treated. He came home in 1973, and amazingly returned to duty, flying Navy jets out of

Miramar, "Fightertown USA," the base featured in the Tom Cruise movie *Top Gun*.

I met him on the *Ocean Pearl* in 1994, by which time he had retired with the rank of captain, and was in demand as an inspirational speaker.

We went to Hanoi together on a shore excursion, in an old Tupelov, a converted Russian bomber. On arrival in the city, we split into different groups.

Mine focused on the military museum opposite a square where soldiers were on parade. And someone slipped away, just like little Tom, running across the road to a warm welcome from the troops. He was a professor and author from a Texas university. That day he must have shaken hands with half the Vietnamese army.

Cole Black also defected from his group, going to a place he knew well — the Hanoi Hilton. Incredibly, the door was open because it was about to be demolished. As Captain Black stepped inside and looked around, an American TV reporter who just happened to be there, thrust a microphone in his face and said something along the lines of "have you been here before?"

A day or two later the interview was shown on national TV in America.

And a phone rang. It was a woman who was wearing a bracelet with his name on it.

When Captain Black returned to the US, the network invited him, and the woman with his bracelet, for a live interview.

Captain Black died in 2007 in a plane crash. He did not spin off the deck of a bucking carrier, or struggle to eject from a shot-up warplane. He was returning from a school where he had delivered a speech aimed at inspiring children, and was flying in a friend's light aircraft, a Piper twin, when it ran out of fuel and crashed.

There are other heroes of the Vietnam War, such as Lee Ellis, a USAF pilot who endured five years of torture and hardship in North Vietnamese POW camps, and managed to return to flying duties.

Colonel Ellis, now retired, has written several books including the best seller, *Leading With Honor: Leadership Lessons from the Hanoi Hilton.* He is a popular lecturer on cruise ships and I met him on a voyage across the Atlantic.

If you are reading this on a cruise ship, now is a good time to check the ship's program. You might find that an inspiring character such as Lee Ellis is about to deliver a talk that could change your life.

THE SHIPS

OCEAN PEARL was built in 1967 by the Wärtsilä shipyard in Helsinki, Finland, as *Finlandia* for the Finland Steamship Company. She entered service for Pearl Cruises as *Pearl of Scandinavia* in 1982. In 1988 she was renamed *Ocean Pearl* and in 1994 was with *Croisières Paquet.* Between 1995 and 1998 she sailed for Costa Cruises as *Costa Playa.* Other owners followed and in 2009 she was sold for scrap to China.

GOLDEN ODYSSEY was built in 1974 for Royal Cruise Line of Piraeus, Greece, at Helsingør, Denmark, and sold in 1989 to Kloster Cruise, Nassau. Later owners called her

Astra II, *Omar II* and she is currently the *Macau Success*, doing overnight gambling cruises from Macau.

ABOUT THE AUTHOR

David Wishart has written for *Cruise Critic*, the *Los Angeles Times*, *New York Post*, *Toronto Star*, *Globe & Mail*, *London Daily Telegraph*, *Financial Times*, *The Times*, *The Independent*, *The Scotsman*, *Bangkok Post*, *New Zealand Herald*, *Essential Marbella* magazine and *Qantas* inflight magazine. He is a member of the Society of American Travel Writers.

His best cruise experiences include standing on the deck of a ship with James Michener, author of *Caribbean*, as the vessel approached the island of San Salvador, believed to be Columbus's first landfall. Others include sailing into Sydney Harbor, and standing under a palm tree in the Caribbean with a cold beer while listening to a steel band. It might have been several beers because he's damned if he can recall which Caribbean island it was.

So why DC Wishart and not David Wishart? Well, there are at least two other established writers called David Wishart. Others, such as JK Rowling and EL James, have got by using initials.

IN CLOSING,

Very many thanks for reading my first novel. I have a good idea for a sequel, so if you enjoyed this one, please let me know and I will get on with it!

You are probably a cruiser, or thinking about your first cruise. Either way, feel free to contact me about any matter relating to cruising. I enjoy ships, being at sea, and talking to people who share my interest.

It would also help me if you would add a comment about my book wherever you purchased my book (if online) or through any of your social media outlets. Thanks very much.

Warm regards,

DC Wishart
Troon, United Kingdom
www.dcwishart.com
www.cruise-plus.com

Lightning Source UK Ltd.
Milton Keynes UK
UKOW06f0000050515

250874UK00024B/269/P

9 780993 151804